API Su~~~~

The Journey to Digital Transformation

Nelson Petracek

Technics Publications

Published by:

2 Lindsley Road, Basking Ridge, NJ 07920 USA
https://www.TechnicsPub.com

Cover design by Josipa Caran Safradin, TIBCO Software Inc.
Chapter contributions by Rob Zazueta

First Printing 2020
Copyright © 2020 by TIBCO Software

ISBN, print ed.	9781634628525
ISBN, Kindle ed.	9781634628532
ISBN, ePub ed.	9781634628549
ISBN, PDF ed.	9781634628556

Library of Congress Control Number: 2020938126

Contents

Acknowledgments

Rob Zazueta, or "Rob Z" as he is typically known, for contributing much of the content at the beginning of the book, and thus laying the foundation for this work.

Maureen Fleming of IDC, who provided her expert guidance and knowledge around the API business model framework.

Salil Kulkarni, EVP & Interim Chief Information Officer, Caesar's Entertainment, for his support, and industry API vision and leadership.

T.M. Ravi, Managing Director, The Hive, for his leadership when it comes to innovation and technology, and for taking the time to review the book while actively participating with the startup community.

Sabeen Ali, CEO and co-founder of AngelHack, for her insights into engaging developers and maintaining a developer community.

Nicole Sanchez and Erin Moeller for their invaluable assistance while I tried to weave this work into my schedule and our many innovative marketing efforts.

Derek Birdsong, Ann Scheurell, and the entire TIBCO creative team, for taking the time to review the content and provide valuable input.

The awesome OOCTO & TIBCO LABS organization, Bob Eve, Shawn Rogers, and the whole team at TIBCO for all of their support.

Thanks to all!

Foreword

Over 20+ years of working together, I've come to see Nelson as one of the best technologists I've ever known. He absorbs pretty much any technology in any category, and advises customers, partners, and internal engineering on the correct architectural context for applying it.

Part of his method for testing scenarios relevant to today's businesses is personally testing all the technology he can get his hands on. He experiments with any given technology independently and integrated with other technologies—all installed on his mainframe of a laptop! And he combines this immersive approach with near-constant face-to-face communications with companies that depend on technology to run their businesses. By applying a clear understanding of what is most important to a business with all he has previously learned and applied, you get one powerful Jedi technologist advising you!

APIs continue to be discussed and written about—and it's easy to understand why when you view how the world, devices (personal and business), and companies have become more and more connected. These connections are now expected in business, and companies can succeed or fail based on their ability to execute the business in real-time. As such, APIs continue to evolve to answer the questions asked and the demands required for success. This evolution necessitates organic changes and innovation. And the organic growth is not just due to advances in technology, but more importantly, due to changes in our way of life and in the way of the connected business. Think about it! ☺

Many API books attempt to push the author's technological approach to building a program and focus way too much on their personal beliefs and favorite technologies. Nelson's philosophy is far more practical and valuable; he sets out the criteria, processes, questions, and thought you need to consider when building and delivering a successful API program. Instead of pushing "the shiny new object," this book will help you understand various technology options and the importance of selecting the technologies which will support maintainability, sustainability, and the goals of your business.

While I firmly believe the entire book contains valuable insight, let me call attention to two chapters that stood out for me: Chapter 5, Building the Business Case for your API Program, and Chapter 14, APIs for the Long Haul.

Chapter 5 underscores the true value of building an API program, supporting the goals of the business, and explains exactly what that means, and most importantly, *how it is accomplished.* Nelson references the Business Model Canvas (BMC) for discovering, documenting, developing, and aligning with the business. While the BMC is a widely accepted approach to documenting business models, Nelson takes it a step further by explaining how you could apply the BCM to building a successful API program, which is far more useful than reading a generic book on the Business Model Canvas itself. Additionally, all the questions he poses will guide those tasked with this phase of API program development. He could have provided answers as well, though that approach most likely wouldn't drive success for the reader. It is imperative that each company document and align value without persuasion or preconceived notions, especially notions that are generic in nature.

Of course, aligning the API program to the business is an absolute must; otherwise, why are you doing it, or more realistically, why would the business care and support it? When alignment and value are attained, take a brief moment to celebrate, but only a brief moment because there's a more vital aspect to be developed: program adaptability and sustainability. Putting it another way, driving a technology-packed, brand new car off the dealer lot is exciting, but without proper maintenance and fuel, it will soon be parked on the side of a road. An API program must be constantly reviewed to keep it maintained, fueled, and running efficiently. Chapter 14, APIs for the Long Haul, examines this critical aspect and provides a fantastic list of questions, by category, for regular check-ups to keep your API machine running with top-notch performance.

Developing an API program is a significant undertaking that can have a profound impact on your organization; it can drive new products, new innovation, new customers, and new revenue streams. Don't worry; in Nelson you have the best API guide possible, and after reading this book, you will undeniably be on your way to a Successful API Journey!

All the best!

Greg James
Chief of Staff, Office of the CTO, TIBCO Software

Introduction

It can be a challenge wading into the world of APIs, whether for the first time or as one moves to an enterprise-wide program.

Back in the mid-2000s, APIs were a relatively new concept, and since documentation was sparse, it didn't take much effort or time to get a lay of the land. There were "only" dozens of articles and a handful of books that tried to cover the basics, as well as a few coding frameworks in various languages promising to build entire APIs—and none of them adequately. Companies like Salesforce, Twitter, and Facebook led the charge, and the conventional wisdom was to follow them.

Since then, APIs have become a legitimate industry unto themselves. The number of conferences focused on APIs has exploded, and just about everyone with more than a modicum of experience has written a book or blog on API "best practices." You'd think this would be a good thing— more information means you can become better informed, right?

Rather than providing clarification, this abundance of information led to many teams becoming mired in debates about standards, frameworks, and best practices that seem meaningful, but are ultimately pointless. Much of the content available, even on topics where you'd expect at least some convergence of opinion, seems more focused on the technical details rather than the overall picture.

> *The reality is everything that needs to be said about APIs and API programs has already been said.*

The problem is, it's said across dozens, even hundreds, of books, articles, conference talks, and more. It's a daunting landscape for those without the time, energy, or interest to track it all but who still need to evaluate the best information and put it into practice.

My goal is to provide you with an "atlas" to guide you and your team to make the right decisions at the right time about how to analyze, plan, design, develop, and market your APIs—whether your target is the open developer community or the engineers down the hall. The advice in this book comes from experience working with many enterprises in overcoming their arguments and obstacles, and subsequently, actually producing APIs that drive value for their business.

That last point is rather crucial. A successful API program is not the sole domain of the engineering and IT teams. Many programs start with the technical teams creating a technical solution to a technical problem, and APIs absolutely fit that need. But that point of view is too narrow. APIs should be designed with the business in mind, even if the primary consumers are the technical teams who created them.

> *Ultimately, APIs are a technical solution to a business problem—how to effectively leverage an organization's data to monetize internal information and processes, rapidly bring new digital products to market, and create new revenue opportunities through partnerships.*

No one team is responsible. A good API program is one that involves several departments, especially the technical, business development, product, and marketing teams. Developers may bristle at this ("they just don't understand the technical challenges!"), and folks on the business side of the house may dread working so closely with their technical peers ("IT just takes so long!"), but there is a tremendous amount of common ground to be found by working together towards a single goal.

It may also surprise business folks to learn that developers often don't have the full picture of why they're building the applications on which they're working. Modern application development paradigms, like Agile methodologies, tend to strike a division between the teams requesting functionality and those tasked with building them. Though Agile intends to drive early feedback from business owners to help ensure active development is heading in the right direction, it also tends to toss user stories and use cases over the wall to engineers without providing much context. This is a major mistake.

Whether you create a "Center of Excellence" or some other cross-functional team structure to support the development of your API program, the crucial point is that you need to involve all of the stakeholders early to ensure every voice is heard and no stone is left unturned.

That's why this book is not directed just towards developers, nor only business development professionals, product managers, marketers, or even executives. It is directed to all of them—as a team. This book gives you the tools and information you and your team need to navigate the complex road of launching and maintaining a successful API program.

CHAPTER 1

Defining the API

How many of us truly understand all facets of an API? As with the parable of the blind men and the elephant,[1] your impression of APIs is likely tainted by how you were first introduced to them:

- If you're a developer or systems architect, you probably think of APIs as a collection of functions provided by some host, either a web application, installed application, or operating system.

- If you're a product manager, you probably think of APIs as a way to share your application data and functionality to allow developers inside and outside your organization to extend the utility of your products.

- If you're an executive or a business analyst, you may think of the value APIs created for major

---

[1] To evaluate a strange animal called an elephant, a group of blind men attempt to know it by touch, and depending on where each touches, discovers that it is "like a thick snake," "like a kind of fan," "a pillar like a tree-trunk," "a wall," "a rope," and "smooth and spear-like."

companies like Salesforce, Facebook, and Twitter by developers in their ecosystems.

Given the focus of this book and its varied audience, I will start with some simple concepts and definitions. For those familiar with APIs and concepts such as HTTP, JSON, and URIs, you may just want to skim this part, and move to subsequent sections of this book. But for those who may be new to these concepts, or wish to have a quick refresher, then this is a great place to start.

APIs are a common way for software programs to get access to the same kinds of information and functionality users can get through a graphical interface.

What makes them seem complex and mysterious is how they combine with other APIs and applications to enable intricate interactions at scale. All modern software development relies on functionality and data provided by other people through shared code libraries compiled locally or hosted on networked systems across the Internet. All of these shared libraries expose an API for programmers to access their content.

But though APIs are technical, their value goes well beyond making the lives of developers a little easier. Well-designed, well-managed APIs are at the heart of any successful digital transformation effort. Where the focus used to be on purchasing and installing the right software to make your company more efficient, the shift is now on creating a platform customized to the needs of the business and made accessible to the right people at the right time in ways that make them productive.

It's all about the Interface

API stands for application programming interface. That "I," interface, to my mind, is the most crucial part. You're familiar with another popular interface for online applications, the web browser. Web browsers and other graphical applications (Microsoft Word, mobile applications, even the calculator app) expose a "human computer interface" or HCI. Just as HCIs target human end users, APIs target applications. If you write a program to consume an API and present its results to a human, you're actually building an HCI from an API.[2]

This book focuses mainly on "web service APIs," that is, those that access content and functions exposed over a network protocol, usually HTTP. Given the popularity and utility of such APIs in recent years, it's difficult to give a more detailed description that genuinely encompasses all of the things an API is capable of doing. You may think of

---

[2] Why do we love acronyms so much in the tech industry? IDK.

APIs as individual HTTP URLs that accept JSON or XML (see *How APIs Work*, below) and return information the same way, typified by the "REST" design pattern. Other API design patterns rely primarily on binary encoding or strictly-formed XML as their preferred data exchange format. Some APIs are invoked over other network protocols like UDP instead of HTTP. And still others are used at the edge of the network, using a completely different set of communications systems, such as Bluetooth.

While our focus here is primarily on APIs that use HTTP, it's important to understand that the same or similar principles apply to just about any API you build for whatever use. More importantly, the lines between systems are blurring as we connect more devices to the Internet. Bluetooth is decidedly not an out of the box Internet-ready protocol, but it's likely you use a Bluetooth-enabled mouse to click links on a web page.

Before APIs: Electronic Data Interchange

APIs are not the only means of interfacing to data and processes, but they are one of the most efficient ways because they allow for better real-time access to information. In the early days of digital business, many industries standardized on a set of methods to exchange large amounts of data such as purchase orders, inventory updates, and customer records via large files. If an update to that data, often called a "delta," was required, a file had to be created and sent over. These files were then uploaded to a server where a process would regularly look for new files and parse and store that information in an internal database.

This form of electronic data exchange is still widely used in some industries, but it carries a great deal of overhead and the lag between collecting, uploading, and parsing the data means it's often out of date before it even gets to the receiving organization's server.

Securely uploading a file to a server, while not difficult, can be surprisingly network and computationally expensive, especially when using older protocols like FTP. The genius of the web is its use of the Hypertext Transfer Protocol (HTTP), which simplifies text file exchanges and allows better interaction with links between documents.

The web was designed first as a publishing platform, a way to create pages that can be read using web browsing software. It took some time before it was also adopted for exchanging text and binary data between machines and programs.

How APIs work: Like a web browser for programs

The web browser is actually a very good analog for how many web service APIs work. At the top of a browser, you'll typically find the URL field. If you want to visit the Google website, you type its address into that box, http://www.google.com. You arrive at the Google homepage, where you can then type in your search request. Clicking the "Google Search" button sends whatever you typed in the box back to Google's servers where it's run through algorithms to discern exactly what it is for which you are searching, and responds with a list of links to related web pages and their descriptions.

A list of links is helpful when you want to visit a web page, but if you're looking for an image, you would type http://www.google.com/imghp (or http://www.google.com/images, which redirects to .../imghp) into your browser. You'll be presented with a similar search field, but the results of your search will be a list of images rather than text links.

In API terms, the Google Image Search URI is a different resource from the main search API. Submitting a search term to Google is sending a request to its servers. The results you get back, whether in the form of links or images, is the response. The data format Google uses in most of its responses is a mix of HTML, Cascading

Stylesheets (CSS), JavaScript, and image data, all of which your browser can interpret and present to you in an attractive and usable format.

If you put a URL for an API resource into your browser, you're likely to see something which looks like it has structure to it, but can be difficult to read. For example, see Figure 1.

Response Body

```
{
    "Class": "Economy",
    "Cost": 100,
    "DepartureDate": "2017-05-27",
    "DeparturePoint": "San Francisco, CA",
    "Destination": "Phoenix, AZ",
    "FirstName": "John",
    "Id": 218991,
    "LastName": "Doe"
}
```

Figure 1. Sample API resource

The weird, oddly structured text is in a format called JavaScript Object Notation or JSON. Where HTML is designed to tell browsers how to lay out the information returned from a server to make it more palatable for a human user, formats like JSON and XML make it easier for applications to read through the data. Even though it has JavaScript in the name, JSON can be easily parsed using just about any programming language running any operating system on any machine with enough power to handle the work.

What APIs do: Agnostic glue

One of the fundamental benefits of web service APIs is that they can work with any programming language in any computer environment with no additional effort.

Unlike code libraries, which must often be provided for each language and each hardware platform separately, most web service APIs allow consumers to use any language, operating system, or hardware, as long as they can connect to a common network.

The value of this openness becomes apparent as you consider how APIs act as the glue in our modern world. Your mobile phone likely contains several applications which are the mobile version of a web application. If you open the same application on your phone and the web browser at the same time, you'll likely see changes made in one show up in the other within seconds.

The creator of that system did not write two completely different versions of the application, they only needed to create the user interfaces for each format, one for the browser, one for the phone. The bulk of the application, the information storage, business logic, user management, and data synchronization, is hosted on backend servers that expose their APIs to the frontend user applications.

Airline Travel Example

A day of travel demonstrates this value even further. When you buy airline tickets, you can use the airline's website or mobile application, or call them directly. You can also book on one of a number of popular travel sites, such as Expedia.com. All of these access the airline's central inventory and ticketing systems through a series of API calls. When you book a ticket, your passenger information is stored in another system shared via APIs with TSA and ground crew at the airport. The systems that scan your boarding pass at security and elsewhere in the airport use APIs to compare the information on your ticket with that provided by the airline.

If your plane is delayed, the airline's scheduling system will call a push notification API to send a message to the airline application on your phone notifying you of the situation. Alternatively, the airline's system can call a telecommunications API that can send an SMS text message directly to your phone number.

When you get to your gate, you can use the airline application on your phone to show your boarding pass as a scannable code and put it face down on the kiosk's monitor. The kiosk makes an API call back to the airline's systems to ensure the ticket is real and valid, and to respond accordingly. Once on the plane, if there are any issues with your reservation, or the airline wishes to offer some kind of personalized service, the flight attendant, using her airline-provided mobile device, can locate your seat.

Once you've arrived at your destination, the airport assigns a baggage claim section to your flight and sends that information to the airline system, which then makes an API call to text you the location of your bags. If you happened to book a hotel with one of the airline's strategic partners, you may also receive a notification welcoming you to your destination and informing you that your room will be ready when you arrive on the property. They, of course, knew your plane arrived because the airline's API provided that information. In this example, APIs powered the exchange of information between the passenger, airline, airport, federal officials, and a trusted partner. The same APIs were accessed by various mobile applications, web browser applications, custom desktop programs, server-based applications, kiosks, and ticketing machines. When the bulk of the business logic in a centralized system is made accessible through APIs, the clients that access them can be thin and focused, which reduces the development costs usually spent in writing software for a new target platform.

As you read this book, you'll see more detailed examples of how APIs have transformed the world and hopefully get inspired to use them to transform your business.

API jargon and conventions in this book

Because APIs are a technical concept, it's difficult to provide a simple definition of them without including a lot of jargon. Your interest and what you need to know about APIs depends largely on your role. While I will do my best to make this topic accessible regardless of your technical level, I will not shy away from the jargon, and neither should you. Get comfortable with it and don't be afraid to dig deeper into a term or concept.

However, even now, there's often not a lot of agreement on what some API terms actually mean. A few basic terms are defined below, and as we proceed throughout this book, I'll do my best to explain any new terms and their meaning in the context of APIs. But for now, this should be sufficient to get us started!

Term	Definition
API	Application programming interface. Code that provides access to a local or network (including cloud) shared library (endpoint) exposing either a series of web services or installed application/data related functions. When combined with other applications, APIs enable intricate interactions at scale.
API Platform	Technical elements and capabilities exposed to developers upon which they can access/buy, define, implement, deploy, manage, and monitor APIs.

Term	Definition
API Program	An initiative that delivers and maintains APIs for a market segment or group, which can involve strategies related to engineering, development, marketing, developer portals, documentation, community engagement, product management, monitoring, security, and more. Some API programs encompass multiple APIs for different endpoint types, such as a user system, a payments system, or an inventory system. A single API program can cover all types to allow for maximum flexibility, reuse, and minimal redundancy. By thinking of APIs in this way, you start to see how they could be used to better serve consuming applications and to expose different combinations of APIs to different groups.
Endpoint	The resource (code library) to which the API allows access.
URI	Uniform resource identifier. A string of characters that unambiguously identifies a particular resource.
URL	Uniform resource locator. A type of uniform resource identifier that specifies a web resource's location on a computer network and a mechanism for retrieving it.
Web Service APIs	APIs that access content and functions exposed over a network protocol, usually HTTP.

CHAPTER 2

Unlocking the Power of Yes with APIs

The technical definition of APIs is helpful only in so far as it describes how APIs work. When you boil it down, APIs are incredibly simple—a way to extract specific data from a server or trigger a function. But this simplicity belies the power of opening access to organizational information in secure ways to control a broad range of interactions with customers, employees, vendors, and partners. I'm passionate about APIs not because of their technical elements, but because of what they enable.

> *Well-designed, well-managed APIs that are concise and secure allow your organization to say "yes" to new opportunities, new markets, and new streams of revenue.*

In the previous chapter, I described APIs from the standpoint of what they are: programmatic interfaces to data and functionality. In this chapter, I demonstrate their business value and what they can accomplish.

The Power of Yes for development projects

As an example of what APIs can do for development projects, let's look at a story which was provided by a former colleague, an API evangelist, and program manager:

Nothing gives me a bigger thrill than being able to say yes to projects when the IT team is leaning toward a no. In one instance, I attended a meeting as an observer with executive leaders to discuss an issue that prevented a large number of our customers from effectively using our browser-based SaaS application. The customer support, sales, and marketing teams pushed for a solution that would represent a fairly radical change in a major part of our user interface.

Our engineering team was already in the midst of a major project to change our underlying systems, which was consuming most of their time and energy. The VP of engineering smirked as he listened to the request of his colleagues and immediately launched into his familiar talk about trade-offs. "Sure, we can build this tool," he said. "Here's the list of everything we're currently working on. What are you willing to delay or kill to get this feature in there?"

This was a "no" thinly disguised as a "yes." Every item on his list had been prioritized as high by all of the executives in the room. The deadline to complete these tasks was firm; future revenue depended on it. The executives eyed each other and their faces turned grim as they realized not only that this request would be held off for at least six months if not a full year, but that all additional requests would also be delayed until the current engineering project was completed.

I love solving problems, and I was already thinking about what it would take to build the feature requested. Knowing our code base and the environment it ran in well, I agreed with the VP of engineering's assessment: building this feature into our current product would require significant effort and delay a vital project. As the manager of our API program, however, I started looking at it with my "API eyes." The functionality and data required for the feature was already available through the same APIs we created to connect our major partners and allow customers to integrate their CRM and ERP systems. Building the user interface for the new feature would take some effort, but there were plenty of open source tools that would make it easier.

I finally alighted on a solution and interrupted the discussion with a bold proclamation: "I can build a proof of concept for this in two weeks with our APIs. If it works, we can just release it as an additional tool and get the same benefits."

The room went quiet. The faces of the marketing and customer support execs brightened with a glimmer of hope. The VP of engineering expressed doubts, stung both by my lack of protocol (I was supposed to just observe and keep my mouth shut in this meeting) and the challenge to the abilities of his engineering team. It would take them months to implement such a solution, he said, even with two or three developers assigned to the task. There's no way I could do it in two weeks on my own.

Challenge accepted: Two weeks later, I delivered the feature using our APIs, hosted on an Amazon Web Services instance using open source software that did everything required. I took an additional two weeks to let our talented graphic design team make it look less like it was designed by a programmer. Then we launched it to the world. The feedback from customers was glowing with praise. And we realized the uplift in revenue we had expected.

The engineering team eventually took what I had built, modified it a bit, then integrated it into the main product, ensuring it would be well documented, supported, and maintained as a key part of our application. More importantly, they adopted an API-led platform approach for future development, focused on exposing the core application through a set of RESTful APIs and building relatively lightweight clients on top to serve our customers across just about any channel they wanted to use.

Everyone loves being a hero. APIs won't get you out of every sticky situation. Still, as this example shows, they can and will allow you and your organization to reply with an emphatic "Yes!" to more opportunities— opportunities to improve your customer experience, experiment with new product features and ideas, build stronger relationships with your strategic partners, and turn your business into an innovation machine that is, if not future proof, at least future tolerant.

The Power of Yes for robot deliveries and interactive TV

The number of APIs you access on a daily basis is staggering, and you probably don't even realize when you use an API. In Chapter 1, I described the flow of the modern connected traveler and how APIs enable them to stay up to date on any changes or interruptions. Flows like this play out again and again in just about every interaction you have with your personal technology.

Every app on your phone that pulls information from a server is doing so using web APIs. When you play a multiplayer game on a console or computer, watch a streaming video on your TV, or order food from a kiosk at a fast food restaurant, you're using APIs.

To get a sense for the utility and ubiquity of APIs, just ask yourself a couple of questions when you interact with digital devices and experiences. "How are APIs enabling this interaction? How could APIs improve it?"

On a recent business trip, I stayed with a leading hotel chain in upstate New York that uses autonomous robots to deliver hospitality items like toiletries and snacks directly to your room. Interacting with these robots is reasonably intuitive. The robot appears at your door, calls your phone, then pops open its cargo compartment so you can retrieve your goods. I haven't spoken with the company who created these, so I don't know for sure how they operate, but I can make some educated guesses.

The interaction starts when a hotel employee receives a request from a guest for an item. The employee locates the item, puts it in the robot's cargo hold, and taps the room number into the onboard screen. The robot then calls a mapping system to calculate the movements it needs to make to get to the room, which is the first place where a set of APIs makes sense. If the robot were to store this mapping information in its own memory and do the calculations itself, it would need to be re-programmed if the room numbers ever changed, if there was some kind of obstruction (a housekeeping cart, new construction), or anything else occurs that would change its programmed route. Storing this information on a server and providing it to the robot via an API would make it easier to apply those changes without requiring a technician to open the machine and replace or update its memory manually.

In this hotel, all of the hotel rooms are above the ground floor, so the robot must take the elevator. It positions itself in front of an elevator but, lacking fingers, it can't press the up or down buttons or the button for the target room's floor. I can only surmise that it's making an API call to the elevator's management system to control the door and buttons.

Once the robot arrives on the correct floor, which it likely knows because the elevator sent it a message through an API, it navigates its way to the room. Onboard sensors keep it from running into people or objects, and it politely moves to one side as people pass. When it reaches the room, it uses a telecommunication API to ring the room's telephone to alert the customer that it has arrived.

There are several ways to implement these interactions that don't use APIs, but many of them are complicated or don't create an optimal experience. Plus, APIs can be repurposed. For example, the APIs the robot uses to call the elevator could also be used by the hotel's app so that guests could call the elevator, see which floor it was on, and receive an estimated wait time before it arrives. The APIs used to ring the room could allow better routing of both internal and in-coming calls and enable caller ID and voice over IP. And the APIs the robot uses to navigate the hotel could be repurposed to provide in-hotel navigation to guests via the giant touchscreen television located in the lobby. In fact, that television is another example of APIs in action. It contains not only information about the hotel, but also about its partners and surrounding businesses. With a simple press, you can find out about local events and even find a flight home. This information comes from third parties like online travel sites, event planning companies, and the scheduling systems of service partners, all delivered via APIs.

Figure 2. API use cases

Once your eyes are opened to these interactions, you start seeing them everywhere. Play this little game and develop your API eyes. Once you start understanding how others are using APIs, the possibilities for your own program will seem limitless.

The Power of Yes for the API platform and program

As you observe API interactions, pay special attention to how those same APIs could be reused for other situations. APIs that provide the airline information displayed on the hotel's interactive screen are likely also driving a travel company's website and providing data for several mobile travel apps. Rather than create a travel information product with a single purpose, the company providing this data has built an API platform that can serve many purposes with little if any additional programming effort needed. This API platform forms the foundation of a successful API program and enables many business capabilities.

Enable new digital products

Many API experts espouse the idea that you should think of your APIs and your API program as products, and their reasoning is sound. Like a product, you need to design, develop, manage, and market APIs throughout their repeating lifecycle. But a good API program is not so much a product as it is an enabler for creating new digital products. Your API program is the foundation on which you build new applications, interactions with customers and software vendors, and more customizable views of your organization's data for better reporting and improved operational efficiency.

The value of thinking of your APIs as a platform rather than a single product should be clear. The same APIs you develop to enact your mobile strategy can be used to integrate with strategic partners or power a kiosk in a retail location. It's hard to imagine any single product that can do all that and more.

You should develop a sense of platform thinking as you approach your API program. The benefits to the long-term health of your business can be tremendous.

Reduce time to market

What does it take for your IT department to develop a new digital product? The standard application lifecycle—design, build, test, deploy, maintain, and improve—gives short shrift to the details of software development, especially the build process. To create a new application, one of the things a developer must first understand is what information will be needed and where it will be sourced.

Often, this information exists in one or more databases, owned by either the company, a vendor, or a partner. For each source of data, the developer must figure out how to gain access and format the data, so it works with the application.

Utilizing the information can be a complicated process involving gaining access to a user account for each datastore. While datastores often have their own user management and rights access systems, they aren't optimized to handle a large number of accounts at a single time. Opening direct access to these systems, especially to developers outside the organization and the network, is complicated and can be challenging to secure. Yet with this approach the process must be completed for every developer and application that needs access.

APIs overcome much of this complexity by exposing information and related functionality through a common set of services that adhere to design best practices. If a developer is seeking a particular piece of data, the IT team can create an API endpoint and control access to it through a single management interface. Anyone else seeking the same data can then easily be granted access. Rather than hunt through system after system to find the data needed, a programmer can visit a developer portal, see the information to which they have access, and using a simple registration process, request a key that unlocks only what the IT team allows.

An API developer portal significantly reduces the time needed to onboard new developers and can dramatically shorten development time, often from months to weeks. Perhaps the most interesting result, though, is how it changes the tone of your digital business.

When the time and cost of building a new digital product drops, so does much of the risk.

Exposing corporate data through secure APIs allows your organization to experiment with new ways to interact with your customers and with your corporate data, and then pursue more opportunities that could turn into long term business. Where the IT organization is often viewed as the gatekeeper to adopting new technologies, taking a platform approach means it can become more of a services organization that takes on a consultative role with technologists both within and outside the organization.

Open new partnership opportunities

Strategic partnerships can add significant value to the business by providing customers with functionality outside your core competency, exposing your product to different markets, and generating shared revenue from the combined marketing and sales efforts of you and your partners. Simple co-marketing partnerships often drive good results when targeting a new market, but the experience can be enhanced when partners share their information in real-time.

Many of the most popular web and mobile applications result from partnerships that allow a company to add functionality to their product using another company's data. Mapping applications, for example, integrate seamlessly with ridesharing applications to make it easy to go from searching for a location to immediately finding a ride. Many customer relationship management applications integrate with email marketing, sales analytics, and social media monitoring companies to provide a more robust customer experience using the same data that drives the core product, all controlled by the owner of that data.

But the possibilities derived from integrating your partners' data don't end there. Exposing a robust set of APIs through your platform creates new opportunities to leverage the corporate data of both companies. Partners can develop interesting ways to work together and grow each other's business, allowing for a stronger relationship and an overall better customer experience.

Maybe you co-create a mobile application targeting a specific audience or use case. Maybe you create interactive advertising campaigns that run both on the web and on a variety of devices popular with your target customers. Or maybe you use each other's APIs to audit and monitor the health of your relationship and seek ways to increase business.

Doing these things with traditional information exchange methods is clunky at best, impossible at worst. Well-designed, well-managed APIs streamline this process and ensure your data is controlled and secured as you pursue new and interesting opportunities.

Enhance the customer experience

Forcing your customers to change their behavior to work with you is a surefire path to stagnant growth. As your audience finds new ways to interact with your organization, you must strive to give them the best, value-generating experience possible, one that motivates them to purchase and inspires loyalty.

Desktop web applications used to be the primary way businesses interacted with their customers. The development of mobile phones and ubiquitous high-speed wireless internet offered new ways to work and connect. But the demands of mobile devices are often dramatically different and usually more restrictive than traditional browser-based applications.

It's possible to create a new product for every device, operating system, and environment that customers want, but the cost to build and support these products would grow to astronomical levels. Reusing data through APIs is far more efficient and allows your organization to tackle a new client application quickly, focusing only on the user experience rather than sourcing new data.

Netflix, widely recognized today as one of the key leaders in the massive digital media space, is an excellent example of this data reuse practice. The Netflix application serves several hundred devices, each with its own quirks and limitations. Most Netflix functionality is made available through fine-grained APIs that cover the entire workflow of logging in, finding something to watch, getting personalized recommendations, and streaming media. By generalizing their APIs, they're able to build a client for new devices in a very short time. To support devices constrained by slower networks or less computational power, Netflix engineers build an intermediary set of services that consume their APIs to offload much of the work from the device. Their API architecture is constantly evolving to better deliver their data to an increasing number of devices, even to those that have yet to be imagined.

Prepare for the future

Perhaps the most valuable aspect of adopting an API platform is in making your organization, if not exactly future proof, at least more future tolerant. There are many threads of technology emerging that point to exciting opportunities, from the creation of small, wearable devices to the possibility of connecting the human mind to computers and attaining the "singularity" championed by technology luminaries such as Ray Kurzweil.

No one can say for sure which new technologies will be true breakthroughs widely adopted by the public. Even the most popular technologies may not be appropriate for your targeted audiences. Your organization must continuously watch the trends and carefully select the avenues that are most likely to lead to more efficient business, better customer experiences, and new revenue opportunities.

A mature API platform and the culture it builds allow you to pursue these opportunities in less time for less cost, reducing risk and increasing the chances of earning a profit. With the right set of services carefully managed and secured, your organization can more easily grow and adapt as market conditions and customer preferences continue to shift.

APIs support your digital transformation strategy

Influential analysts and consultants have for several years now been urging companies to undergo a digital transformation. It's likely you're developing an API strategy as a key part of your own transformation. The purpose of going digital is to intelligently use technology to improve your internal processes and gain better access to corporate data, all in the name of becoming a more efficient organization. In this, APIs are clearly a smart path forward. But as aligned as your API strategy can be to your transformation efforts, it's important not to adopt a technology simply to check a box.

A solid digital strategy starts by reviewing your organization's key processes and evaluating their accessibility, control, monitoring, and metrics. Once you have a strong understanding of these factors, you can adjust your API strategy and program to address any gaps and take advantage of your strengths.

Accessibility

Each manager in your organization should review both the processes they own directly and those they contribute, to ensure everyone who needs access to the processes and the information they capture has it. More importantly, managers should review how access is granted and how difficult it is to provide it to new employees.

Accessibility is the main area where a consistent API strategy can help your organization at its core. APIs can make corporate data accessible in a common format that can easily be used by applications, analytics tools, and integration systems —and provide that access in a secure way that adheres to your business rules and requirements.

Control

While easy accessibility to corporate data is a desirable outcome, you need to ensure your most sensitive and proprietary information remains protected. That means all requests for digital corporate assets must be authenticated to ensure the user making the request is who they say they are.

Once authenticated, the system should also automatically ensure the user is authorized to access the requested data in accordance with your corporate governance policies. A digital approach to this kind of control not only automates the process, but it can also allow for more intricate rules and requirements. A best practice, in this case, is to centralize authentication (the aspect that positively identifies a user) and localize authorization, allowing individual applications and systems to control who is allowed to access their data and functionality. Good API management tools and gateways paired with a best of breed authentication server can handle the heavy lifting.

Monitoring

It can be difficult to impossible to get much visibility into non-digital processes. If your processes are mostly ad hoc and merely shuffle data around rather than integrate and enforce workflows, inefficiencies can rapidly form and systems can break down. As a start, digital process automation tools can help you standardize, enforce, and automate processes, freeing your teams to spend more time delivering value to customers, and less time checking and following procedures.

But one of the most critical aspects of a digital transformation program is visibility into these processes and functions. With so many systems emitting data, it can be difficult to understand where things are flowing and when to react. This is also where APIs can help. Visualization tools can help make sense of API-enabled process data and identify patterns to track. Real-time business event processing tools can identify when a predetermined set of events occurs and utilize APIs to trigger an automatic reaction, including calling on human intervention when necessary, to bring some order to chaos.

Real-time analysis of web and API server logs can also surface insights and event patterns for improving system performance, customer experience, and employee efficiency and effectiveness.

Metrics

None of this work matters, however, if you're not driving toward business goals. Monitoring your systems in real time can keep everything running smoothly, but tracking your key performance metrics against goals allows for better decisions, increased business growth, and identification of new opportunities that may not at first be obvious.

Successful digital companies build a culture of metrics-driven decision-making across all levels and all departments. Knowing the numbers to watch, and how they influence the rest of the business, gives each employee a clear path to the needs of the business and their own individual success. Many express the concern that a business driven by metrics alone leaves no room for the kind of intuition, creativity, and gut instinct indicative of visionary leaders. On the contrary, a more efficient organization means you can take more risks with less effort and lower cost. A culture that values transparent access to corporate KPIs can help identify which risks have paid off and point the path forward to new opportunities.

Building a metrics-driven culture starts with defining and understanding your corporate goals, both at a macro level and the level of individual campaigns and projects. Understanding these goals will help you design digital programs that better fit your company's culture and targeted customers. Spending the time early in your API planning to define these goals and their associated metrics will set you up for long term success.

Final thoughts

APIs are more than just a technology. A strong foundation of APIs created with a platform mindset can drive business value, open up new avenues for revenue, strengthen partner relationships, and enable a compelling experience for your customers both now and in the future. No digital transformation strategy should be without them, as the process of developing your API strategy will also result in improvements to your underlying data and processes, and unlock the true potential of your organization.

CHAPTER 3

Making Money and Measuring Success

One true measure of the success of your API program is how well it addresses and drives toward the goals of the business. And what are the goals of the business? **TO MAKE MONEY!**

It may seem strange to think of APIs as revenue-generating, especially if your perspective is from the technical side. But doing so not only helps convince key stakeholders and executives to fund your program, it brings focus and enlightenment to every decision made in the process. It's one thing to design and deploy an API to address a particular use case. It's another thing entirely to know how that API is reducing costs, improving development time, or driving revenue, whether directly or indirectly. These factors will influence how to design, reuse, and expose your APIs.

Several metrics assess API program success, including the number of API calls, the number of active developers or users, and others. These metrics help you monitor performance and indicate how well your marketing and management efforts are working. Still, none are as crucial to the business as how much money your API program is generating or saving your company.

Charge for Access	Value Adds And Upsells	Driving Revenue Generating Activities	Forging Strategic Partnerships	Improving Operational Efficiency
Charge per call or subscription. — — — Works well for companies providing data services.	Position at "Silver level and above" tiers. — — — Useful for SaaS businesses and customers that want custom integration.	Use for affiliate programs, marketing automation. — — — Ideal for e-commerce.	Share data and functionality with partners. — — — Share revenue with partners. — — — Increase exposure to partner customer base.	Quickly respond to market changes. — — — Adapt to new technologies. — — — Improve time to market.
Examples:	Examples:	Examples:	Examples:	Examples:
Sportsradar Rovi	Salesforce	Amazon Shopify	Uber Pinterest	Argos Comcast Netflix

Figure 3. Five typical API monetization models

It's worth taking the time in the planning stages to think this through, well before you write a single line of code, as it will help influence a number of the decisions you'll need to make along the way. Working with companies of all sizes across all industries in numerous technology areas,

I've encountered five typical API monetization models that succinctly demonstrate the value an API program can bring to the business and can be used to point the way forward.

These models can help you zero in on how to start designing your program and focus the team's attention on driving toward the goals of the business. The models, left to right, are from most to least direct monetization. But a successful program does not need to be limited to only one of them; some of the best API programs I've seen leverage several of these models, in some cases, while targeting the same audiences.

Metrics and program design

As discussed, it is critical to understand how your APIs can drive value for the business, but it's even more important to measure how well they're doing it. Each monetization model has its own metrics to build into your program at the time of launch.

Some of the metrics reporting can come from the systems you use to create, host, and manage your APIs, but much of the data will need to come from other sources, such as your customer relationship management (CRM) systems, billing systems, and even your internal technical planning tools. In some cases, you will need to design processes to ensure that the appropriate data is being collected and correlated in the right ways. Business intelligence tools can help a great deal with this, but you must plan for this collection and analysis at the same time you're designing your program. Waiting until after your program is launched will likely result in the loss of valuable data that could have helped point your team toward ways to improve your program and drive more business.

Each model's metrics are slightly different, but most of them reflect the same principle: follow the money. It's fairly easy to do when the monetization is more direct, especially when real money is changing hands. However, it can be difficult to define when no price is attached to a set of API calls. As you consider these models, think through the systems you already have that track other related metrics and how you might be able to tie that data to the goals of your API program.

All of the models that serve an external API consumer need to track the average revenue per user (ARPU) and lifetime value of the customer (LTV). These are common metrics, and it is likely that you are already tracking these metrics elsewhere in your organization to assess the success of other products.

ARPU helps you understand the rough value of each user over a specific period. It is calculated by simply taking the revenue generated by your API program during the time period on which you're focusing—month, quarter, year—and dividing by the number of active users during that same period. For best results, it's useful to define active users as those who have an account they could have accessed during that period of time, whether they actually logged in or not. If, for example, your program generated $150,000 in 2020 and you had 5,000 active users during the year, your ARPU for 2020 is $30. Comparing this to the average cost per user should give you an idea of your profitability. Segmenting your audience further and measuring their relative ARPUs can show you which audiences are most valuable and, thus, should be the targets of your marketing efforts.

LTV is a similar calculation, but over the entire lifetime of a customer. You traditionally calculate LTV by determining the average purchase price of your products and multiplying by the average number of times a customer makes a purchase over their lifetime with you. Since many API programs are tied to some kind of recurring revenue model, it may be more helpful to calculate the ARPU per month and multiply that by the average number of months between when a customer starts paying and when they churn out. Regardless of how you choose to calculate it, make sure it follows the same principle and guidelines as the rest of your internal accounting so you can arrive at numbers that are compatible with one another.

Determining LTV is especially useful when you are budgeting for marketing activities. To maintain profitability, the average cost to acquire a customer (CAC) should be less than the average LTV.

The golden rule for all business metrics is to identify those numbers that demonstrate how well you are performing against your stated goals.

LTV, ARPU, CAC, and others are generally accepted metrics, but don't be afraid to create new ones if you're measuring something specific. The metrics recommended in each model are guidelines, and you'd do well to measure them, but it pays to establish a long-term data gathering and analytics practice that continually answers questions about performance. Define your goals, determine what success looks like to you, and then put the right tools in place to measure how well you're succeeding against your expectations.

The five API monetization models

Model 1: Charge for access

When most organizations talk about monetizing their APIs, they start by considering charging directly for access, either per-call or per subscription. Choosing the Charge for Access model first makes sense; it's the model that's easiest to understand and easiest to track. You can simply look at your income reports to determine the success of your program and adjust prices and marketing efforts to target various audiences.

Though this model is the easiest to measure, it tends to be the most challenging to implement. If the data or functionality you're providing through your APIs has clear monetizable value, then charging directly for that access makes sense. But this is not a determination that you and your team can easily make. Like any product in the open market, it's up to customers to determine its value.

Far too many executives have told me that API products just don't work because no one is willing to pay for them. That's simply not true; it's that no one was willing to pay for *their* APIs. Perhaps it's because they didn't understand how to market to their target audiences. Maybe they had a poor design that caused too many difficulties. In most cases, though, they simply overestimated the value of their data or exposed functions.

To be successful with this approach, you must carefully consider your target audience, the goals of your business, and the value of your APIs to the audience. If the purpose of your API program is to provide data and functionality that you would otherwise sell or provide in other formats to the open market, you likely have a good case for direct monetization. However, if you design APIs to provide value through third-party integrations, you may want to consider other models.

Sportradar built its business by supplying reliable, real-time sports statistics to media companies, sports applications, and other digital sports channels. It provides clear pricing tiers targeting different customer needs. In most cases, a customer can sign up, provide payment information, and begin accessing data immediately. Sportradar is a model example of successful direct monetization.

There's a real possibility that your primary APIs may not be directly monetizable, but there may still be proprietary data you control that can be valuable to others. For example, I've heard of a cloud-based supply-chain management company that used APIs and an upsell model to provide different levels of access to the software. To ensure delivery and ordering modules were as accurate as possible, they had a team of people who carefully tracked every location for every store, warehouse, and facility their customers used. Starbucks, for example, opens and closes stores so often that any list of currently operating stores will rapidly become obsolete. It was the goal of this team to keep track of such lists for all of their customers independent of their customers' lists, which meant the supply chain software was often more accurate than their customers' data.

These up-to-date lists provided tremendous value not only for their customers but also for mapping companies like Google that struggled to keep this information accurate. The supply chain company was already paying their staff to maintain this list, but they found an additional revenue stream by exposing the list as a read-only API to third-party companies, many of whom were not their traditional customers. It was a small amount of effort to do this, so any revenue was practically pure profit.

What kinds of data does your company have that you may be able to provide for a fee without giving up your competitive advantage?

Pricing your APIs

Because APIs are not tangible products, pricing them can be a challenge for companies that don't sell software.

Price products to make a profit—you cover the cost of the parts, labor, marketing, and distribution, set a profit margin, and you have your price.

The cost of developing, hosting, and supporting your APIs may already be built into your IT budget, especially if you follow the best practice of having your internal teams use the same set of APIs your customers use.

One simplistic but effective way to figure out the cost of hosting your API is to look at the run costs of the system supporting it, including bandwidth charges, server hosting/cloud fees, equipment costs, and administrative labor costs. Or, if your entire system is API-led, look at your total IT budget and divide by the number of calls or operations your system is capable of supporting. The chances are your IT teams already have this number because they need it to plan for capacity.

You can use this cost-per-call number to budget for your expected growth needs for supporting a wider audience and as the basis for your pricing decisions. Remember to refresh your cost-per-call estimate frequently to compensate for any changes introduced by re-architecting your system or moving to different infrastructure providers.

The next step is to understand the price to which your target market will respond. Review what similar API programs or other services charge and see how your cost-per-call plus profit margin expectations stack up. If your prices are higher than average, promote the unique value your APIs offer. When selling to developers, a topic covered in detail during Chapter 8, the two greatest values they look for are ease of use and breadth and uniqueness of functionality. If you can make their jobs easier and reduce development time for a reasonable cost, you'll win their business every time.

Keep in mind that your end-users are rarely the ones who make the purchasing decision. Developers will make recommendations to their management teams, who will find money in the budget to make the necessary purchases.

> *Arm both your sales team and your developer customers with the right messaging, knowledge, and value proposition to help them convince their management that you're worth the purchase.*

How you charge for access has a lot of influence over your actual pricing. In the direct monetization model, there are two ways to charge for access: per-call or through recurrently billed subscription tiers.

Per-call pricing

The benefit of per-call pricing is that you can easily account for revenue. If each call costs your team $0.005, and you charge $0.01 per call, you can see where profit starts, which makes it easy to forecast revenue based on traffic patterns.

But this ease can come at a high cost to your customers. It's difficult to estimate how many calls any application will have to make, which complicates cost forecasting. APIs that require more calls for simple functionality (aka "chatty" APIs), cost more than those with an efficient design. The cost-per-call figure is also not usually consistent across all API calls; some require more data transfer or CPU power than others, which leads to uneven expectations in revenue reporting. Complicating all this are changes to API design best practices. The GraphQL API format, which allows for greater client control over the amount of data requested and returned in a single call, breaks the per-call pricing model completely. Per-data (per kilobyte, per megabyte) pricing models are similarly complicated for many of the same reasons.

Tiered subscription pricing

Subscription tiers offer a better way to charge directly for data by allowing customers to better predict their costs based on fixed pricing and the average cost per call across a larger pool. This approach minimizes revenue fluctuations across different usage profiles for different endpoints.

As you research your target market and its pricing sensitivity, segment it into three to five distinct groups. These groups form the basis of your pricing tiers.

To help decide on exact pricing, ask your team:

- How many calls might we expect applications built by customers in each tier to make per month?
- How valuable are our APIs to the success of each tier's applications?
- How much revenue do we expect their applications to make for them?

- What are the estimated costs associated with these tiers using our cost per call number?
- What is our estimated cost at the top of the range of each tier vs. the bottom?
- What is our estimated cost across the entire spectrum of each tier?

For each of these questions and answers, define how you will calculate the metric and how you intend to use it. The answers to these questions will help you make better pricing decisions to arrive at reasonable and affordable pricing for customers while generating a steady profit for the business.

Measuring success

In this Charge for Access model, your APIs are products and should be measured and managed accordingly. When developers register for access, make sure you're asking questions that can help categorize them into useful demographic segments, such as the industry for which they work, the type of development they typically perform, and the audience they're targeting. You can also segment by the number of calls per month, types of calls made, and anything else that helps make sense of the usage patterns you're seeing.

This segmentation is particularly helpful when directly monetizing your APIs because it can influence the approaches used to grow revenue, including allowing you to target your most valued audiences or hi-lighting how you can change tactics to drive the behavior of other customers. Your ARPU and LTV metrics are especially helpful here.

If you're working in a subscription model, looking at your recurring revenue, the amount of money generated in total by these subscriptions, can give a general overview of the health of the business. In particular, monthly recurring revenue can help you quickly gauge how well your marketing and growth efforts are performing.

In all cases of direct monetization, you'll want to pay special attention to how much time it takes a new customer to go from signup to their first API call. Ideally, this should be a matter of mere minutes, but approval queues, complicated documentation, and onboarding processes can all slow this down, reducing your overall time to revenue. Determining how you're performing on this item can be as easy as capturing the date and time that a user first requested access, and comparing it to the date and time at each step in your approval process, as well as to the date and time of their first call.

Model 2: Value adds and upsells

APIs designed with the customer of your existing software platform or service in mind are quite valuable; they provide a layer of customization and usability to the customer with a low amount of effort. However, charging for these APIs directly, in addition to charging for another account on your SaaS platform, for example, may leave many of your customers cold.

If the goal of your API program is to add value and increased functionality for customers, consider either including API access as part of your standard user subscription at no extra charge or creating different user tiers with API access included at the higher tiers.

Opening your APIs to existing customers for free makes sense when you establish your API program to increase customer loyalty and stickiness, especially when your customers are clamoring for programmatic access to the data and functions they use in your applications. While it can be challenging to track the revenue flowing through your API, you can compare usage to the revenues generated by the accounts using the API to get an idea of how much money it's earning.

Adding API access as a feature at higher user account levels can be an attractive benefit for those seeking a bit more functionality and customization. This approach generally works best for web applications and companies that already sell their services through various subscription tiers. Where your lowest tier may offer basic access to your applications with some limitations, higher tiers may offer additional benefits, such as greater access to existing features, exclusive access to non-basic functions, and even access to your APIs.

Salesforce is the classic early example of this kind of tiered account. When Salesforce first started offering API access to customers, it was available as a feature for those who purchased third-tier access and above, whether customers explicitly asked for it or not. This opened the API to the most dedicated set of customers and forced those in the lower tiers to consider what access to the API might be worth to them, allowing the teams supporting Salesforce's APIs to focus their attention on actual customer integrations rather than dozens or hundreds of proof of concept applications built by the open market. Salesforce also built and maintained its AppExchange to allow third-party developers to integrate with Salesforce customers through a tightly managed process that has proven beneficial to all players.

Salesforce still allows customization through its APIs at the third tier (called Lightning Enterprise), while opening limited access at lower tiers as well, allowing for greater but finer-grained control over API access based on customer type and general use case.

Measuring the success of upselling API programs requires looking at the customers and revenues in those tiers. The revenue generated through accounts actively using the

API should be compared to the rest of the cohort to get an even clearer picture.

Measuring success

The challenge in measuring the success of an upsell is understanding what prompted the customer to make the purchase, especially if the upsold account has more than API access as an added feature. One way to mitigate this is to compare the total number of users at the upsold level to the cohort in that same level that has actively called the API. If, say, only 20% of your customers at the API level are actively calling the API, it's likely not as valued by this cohort, and you may want to consider changing your subscription structures.

Model 3: Driving revenue-generating activities

Web applications are typically optimized to drive customers toward a specific revenue-generating activity, such as purchasing a product, booking a service, or completing an action. Often, the consumers of these APIs receive some percentage of revenue for every sale they close. Offering the API for free to these users encourages adoption and experimentation, all to improve sales.

If you adopt this model, design your APIs to drive these revenue-generating activities. Users should be able to easily search through your available inventory with well-defined criteria that help them narrow their results to only those items that most closely match what they're looking for. The process from search to selection to payment should be as efficient as possible to reduce any sales friction.

Measuring success

Since generating revenue with this model only occurs when certain API calls are made or processes are completed, you need to determine what those calls and processes are and attach revenue numbers to them. For example, if you design your API to drive online product sales, you may only make money when a successful call to charge the customer and complete the order is made. Record the amount collected and tally those numbers to measure the success of your efforts.

If your web application uses the same set of APIs as other customers, you'll want to ensure you attribute each sale to a developer key. Then, separate the internal keys from the external keys to understand which sales are made by your application and which are the result of external API calls.

Often, the compute costs involved in searching for products, especially those with complex parameters and relationships within the system, are the most expensive cost component. As a result, programs with a high "look to book" ratio, which is a large number of searches compared to the number of successful purchases, can affect profitability. Measure this number regularly and look for ways to optimize your search capabilities, drive down compute costs, and subsequently improve overall profitability.

Model 4: Forging strategic partnerships

Strategic partnerships are an ideal way to expand your reach and capabilities with minimal cost and without losing focus on your core competencies. These partnerships often take the form of co-marketing and co-selling, especially in the online business space. In this model, strategic partners can share data, better integrate each other's functionality, and form a more cohesive experience by consuming each other's APIs.

Examples include embedding partner functionality into your application to make it available to your customers, passing a user's data held by a partner into your system for easy integration, or even co-marketing using a shared database of customers carefully segmented using the additional information provided by your partners. Most of these partnerships will be structured to split revenue as a vendor-client relationship or to expand market exposure for each company.

Regardless of the type of partnership, make sure you're putting the right tracking and reporting in place early and that both parties agree on and share the KPIs that are specific to each business. Having these values in place ensures that both parties agree on expectations and that each can react quickly when the metrics don't match these expectations.

Measuring success

Both parties to a strategic partnership should be clear as to their expectations and goals for working together. Any established contract will likely enshrine much of this and should be the primary guide as you determine what metrics to follow to ensure both parties are seeing success. Results should be shared often to help the partnership grow.

Your own goals for the partnership, however, may extend beyond the contract. If the primary purpose of the partnership is to drive new revenue that you both split, you'll want to pay close attention to how your specific efforts outside those of your partners are helping. If you intend to grow your market by exposing your products and services to that of your partners, you'll want to measure your overall share of voice in the marketplace. This is a complicated metric that requires tracking mentions on social media and in the press, and processing this data with semantic analysis.

As with all business models, make sure you clearly understand your goals, know what success should look like, and put the right tracking in place to regularly check those metrics.

Model 5: Improving operational efficiency

When open ecosystem APIs using RESTful web services first hit the market, developers were thrilled by the amount of data, functionality, and ease of access newly available to them. These APIs did not lock them into specific languages, frameworks, or environments, so they could build applications using tools with which they were most comfortable.

An interesting side effect of this ecosystem was that the developers who produced those APIs grew jealous of how easy their developer customers had it. Where a third-party developer could easily access JSON-formatted data through a simple RESTful interface, most internal development still required proprietary or legacy techniques and direct connection to the code bases and systems they were accessing. This led to dependencies that slowed development.

In the early days, it took some convincing for IT departments to begin abstracting their internal services and offering them as APIs. Today, it's considered a best practice with the highest return on investment.

Adopting API-first development practices can significantly reduce time to market for new digital products, often from months to weeks. These improved efficiencies have benefits that go far beyond cost savings, though they can be significant. When it costs less to produce mature applications in less time, it's easier to try things that might otherwise be considered risky. For example, if someone on the executive team thinks a virtual reality client may generate revenue, a simple cost analysis will demonstrate that the bulk of the budget would go into developing the actual client application, with much of the server side being provided by APIs, many of which may have already been deployed. These APIs reduce development cost and risk, making such experiments more affordable and creating a culture of innovation that can increase revenues while invigorating the creativity of your staff.

APIs help companies like Netflix support many clients with many different needs. APIs are layered at varying places in the technology stack to allow communication between services running on countless machines. API-related patterns such as the Backend for Frontend (BFF) pattern enable more efficient communication over limited channels without sacrificing service reusability. In the modern architecture stack, it's practically APIs all the way down, with tremendous gains to be made from reducing technical debt, reducing time-to-market for new products, and improving developer onboarding.

Measuring success

It can be challenging to tie revenue directly back to this type of internal development. The benefits are typically derived from your ability to easily improve existing products while rapidly experimenting with new ideas that may themselves eventually generate revenue.

With this model, establish a set of baseline metrics to understand how well your development team is performing today:

- What is the average time required to bring a product to market from idea to deployment?
- How much development time is spent on these products on average?
- How long does it take for a newly hired developer to become genuinely productive?

Establishing these metrics early will help you refine your internal processes and better leverage your APIs to improve overall time to market.

Beyond the engineering organization, however, APIs can also help the entire company become an innovation machine. Too often, good ideas are shelved because they take engineering focus away from core product and business needs. Companies that adopt a more innovative stance, however, can take more risks for less money and zero in on better product-market fit much faster. Measuring the rate of innovation in your company requires a deep understanding of what innovation looks like for you and how it contributes to your goals.

Final thoughts

Regardless of which of the five monetization models you choose for your program (and remember, you can select combinations of these models), it is vital to start as early as possible to define how your APIs will help the organization meet its goals. This definition, along with a cohesive monitoring and metrics collection strategy, will help shape the execution of your program, keep stakeholders informed, and ensure that you are making the desired impact.

CHAPTER 4

Staffing Your API Program

There was a time not long ago when APIs were rather esoteric, requiring specialized knowledge that was not easy to come by without direct experience. This created a bit of a chicken and egg problem when it came to developing skills but, as APIs have matured, this problem has slowly disappeared. While API specialists are still valued, you should expect more of your employees to absorb the skills and thinking necessary to make your API program a success. The more that people in your organization know about your APIs and the value they bring both to the company and your customers, the more your organization can capitalize on the opportunities they present.

Even if you are just starting on your API journey, chances are good you already have many of the right people in place to make it successful. While you can build a team focused entirely on developing and managing your API program, which may be ideal in the beginning, you will likely find it more valuable to integrate API skills into more of your departments and business processes in a way that makes APIs less "special" and more integral to the operation of the business.

Rather than focusing on the positions for which to hire, consider instead the roles you should fill.

This chapter discusses a number of these roles and responsibilities, and is intended to act as a reference and precursor to building the business case behind your program. Some of these roles are highlighted in Figure 4.

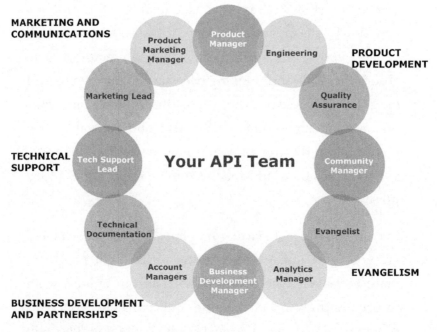

Figure 4. Roles and responsibilities

The roles you need to fill will be dependent on the goals of your program and who you are targeting. But even an internal API program focused solely on improved integration should seek to cover all of the bases, including marketing and communication, for the best chances of success. Use the roles as guidelines, not job descriptions. How you ultimately fill these roles depends on how you've designed your program.

Product development

If you follow the best practice of integrating APIs into every aspect of your digital product development, the product development roles will be filled by your existing staff. Still, it's essential to understand who owns what aspects of developing and maintaining the APIs, and to communicate that clearly among your team, so everyone knows who to turn to with questions and new opportunities. If you're building an API team from scratch, however, you'll want to carefully cover each of these technical roles to ensure your success.

Product manager

While building the platform to support your APIs and new digital business, you'll want to ensure you manage each API as a product. The product manager (PM) is often considered the CEO of the products they manage: the product's success is their success, and the product's inadequacies are theirs to fix.

The product manager, therefore, is the ringmaster for the three-ring circus that is your API program. They must define the target audiences, understand them intimately, and ensure every aspect of the product experience addresses the needs of customers while also serving the goals of the business. A good product manager is one who has strong technical knowledge equal to their business prowess.

The product manager will own the roadmap, help coordinate the development process, drive the top-level marketing agenda, and check in regularly with all stakeholders, including customers, to ensure needs are being met and opportunities for growth and improvement are not left behind. It's an exhausting but exhilarating role that can springboard an entire career.

Enterprise architect

If the product manager is the ringleader of the circus, the enterprise architect is both the lion tamer and the show coordinator. This is a role traditionally found in larger IT operations teams that is focused on defining the software, environments, hardware, and other systems that run the company. Traditionally, this role has acted as the gatekeeper for new technologies, ensuring they mesh well with existing systems and are keeping costs as low as possible. Enterprise architects have, therefore, often earned the reputation as "the Managers of No."

In an API-first environment, however, this role becomes more consultative. The enterprise architect must still maintain technical standards and ensure core systems operate efficiently and effectively, but exposing corporate data and functionality through APIs allows them to maintain data security and consistency without tremendous overhead. As a result, the enterprise architect is often the arbiter who defines and controls internal API style guidelines, standards, and best practices, and works with other teams to ensure they adhere to those rules. As the API program grows and needs changes, this role is responsible for scaling the underlying systems and ensuring they remain performant.

The role of managing the APIs—controlling access, packaging endpoints to target specific audiences, and monitoring performance—is often split between the enterprise architect and the product manager, each focused primarily on their own areas of concern.

Software engineers

Modern web and cloud-native development practices emphasize the flexibility and modularity APIs provide, so many software engineers already have the basic knowledge necessary to create new APIs from code. Where there is some debate—and still some poorly distributed knowledge and experience— is how best to expose APIs following popular styles, such as REST, GraphQL, gRPC, and others.

Software engineers are front line technical experts who may know their code inside and out, but may not always have the bigger picture. It's important to engage your engineers as you design and plan your APIs and get their feedback early in the process. Still, the role of finalizing style guidelines and enforcing them should rest with either the enterprise architect or another engineering manager. Software engineers should follow those guidelines, straying only when necessary and only after having discussed it with the enterprise architect.

Quality assurance/Devops engineers

Software test automation has revolutionized software deployment. New code used to be gathered for weeks or even months until it could be rolled out to production in one big deployment along with dozens or hundreds of other changes. Even the smallest change, such as fixing a typo on a web page, often had to wait until a major release. While many organizations still adhere to these types of processes, they are fraught with challenges that can cause an engineering team to stop all work when a bug inevitably slips through.

The concept of "DevOps," an amalgam of development and IT operations, has made code deployments far more efficient. New code can be released often, even several times a day, and with less risk, as releasing a hotfix for a bug can occur within hours rather than weeks or months. Many quality assurance (QA) engineers, who used to focus on testing scripts as they manually poked each piece of code to tease out any deficiencies, have adopted automated testing tools and become DevOps engineers. In this role, the engineers focus less on testing code and more on building environments that automate as much of the build-test-deploy process as possible.

The code that exposes your APIs, as well as the APIs themselves, needs to be part of your overall testing plan, and this plan integrates into your DevOps processes. Your DevOps engineers should be well-versed in these tools and work with software engineers to build a system that makes it easy to deploy solid APIs.

Technical support

Technical support for APIs is much different than most other support tasks. Since your primary end user will typically be a developer of some kind, your API technical support team must be at least as technical as your customers, and capable of helping programmers regardless of the language or environment they use.

Tech support lead

Most technical support departments have multiple layers that provide differing levels of support. Tier one support, for example, is often provided by less technically knowledgeable staff who follow a series of scripts or rely on a knowledge base to address customer issues. In an API program, however, many customer issues will require your support team to look at the customer's code to understand what they're trying to do and identify where they may have made a mistake. Should a technical customer contact your API support team and discover they aren't quite up to the task, that creates a poor developer experience that can reflect poorly on your entire program.

The tech support lead, therefore, needs to be focused on identifying the right people to address developer needs and build a team and a set of processes that can help customers as efficiently as possible. They must also ensure that developer support documentation is up to date, written clearly, and addresses the most common questions received from customers.

Developer site manager

The developer portal is a key piece of your developer experience. It's the source of truth for all information regarding your APIs and must be kept up to date alongside the APIs themselves. The developer site manager is responsible for keeping the portal performant and up to date, and for working with the software engineering team to streamline the process of taking their documentation and making it readable and appropriate for the target audiences.

The developer site manager may also find new and interesting ways to make it easier for customers to start using your APIs, including managing software development kits, sample code, and any other assets that make the developer portal a more valuable resource.

Marketing and communications

If your program is not externally focused on strategic partners and third-party developers, you may be tempted to believe you don't need to consider building a marketing plan. But introducing new development ideas into an organization can sometimes be more difficult than driving new customers to your products. While your program may not require a full-blown marketing team, you'll still want to pay attention to the roles listed below and find ways to address what they cover as you evangelize your program internally.

Product marketing manager

The product marketing manager (PMM) often acts as the marketing lead for your API program. They are responsible for setting the strategy as to how the value of your program will be communicated to your target audience, and for helping to execute against that plan. In many cases, your PMM will be a shared resource with the marketing team, and thus also likely responsible for other digital products you produce in your organization.

Technical writer

Developers are not known to be the best communicators, but communicating to them is critical. While all of your API documentation should start with the developers who build the APIs themselves, a technical writer can help make that documentation more readable and accessible to a wider audience. Strong writing skills are required, of course, but so is some level of technical knowledge to make better sense of what your development team is trying to describe.

Business development and partnerships

If your program is externally facing, whether targeting the open ecosystem, strategic partners, or even just your vendors, you'll want business development managers setting the strategy for those engagements and ensuring the program is performing against its goals. If your organization already has a channel partner strategy, you likely have this team in place. They should be included in any of your high-level conversations about your API programs, and asked to provide their input on how to best serve the needs of your partners.

Business development lead

The business development lead (BD lead) is typically a director or higher-level person charged with setting and executing on a channel partner strategy. Though not necessarily directly involved with your API program, this role should help guide your decisions as you define your target audiences and the services you will expose.

The BD lead either commands a small team of salespeople dedicated to qualifying and signing partnerships, or works closely with the enterprise sales team to identify partnership opportunities through their prospecting efforts. As a result, the BD lead, along with the product marketing manager, often also sets the sales strategy for getting your services into the hands of your customers and partners. Involve the BD lead in the earliest stages of your program's development and keep them in the loop throughout development. Once launched, the BD lead is likely to become one of your strongest advocates on the business side of the organization.

Account managers

As you sign new partners and they implement your services, you'll want to provide a certain level of "white glove" service to the most strategic and valuable among them. The account manager manages the business side of this partner relationship and acts as a single point of contact for the partners they support, often delegating questions to the correct technical support and engineering people as needed.

The account manager not only helps address partner questions and issues, but they also help ensure the accounts they represent are performing against the goals stated in the partnership. These goals should have measurable key performance indicator metrics, and be agreed to by all parties to ensure the partnership is working as anticipated. If the metrics aren't lining up or if different metrics may better measure success, the account manager should act quickly to address those issues.

Evangelism

It may seem strange to think of technical marketing as "evangelism." The word evokes scenes of crowded tents on a Sunday morning presided over by a charismatic preacher promising to save every last soul. But that's exactly the vision you should have when you think of technical evangelism. Rather than a spiritual revival, technical evangelism tries to capture and spread the excitement felt by many developers and technical experts as they build new and fascinating products that change the ways we work and live. In terms of your API program, you should think of evangelist activities as bringing as many people into your tent as possible to spread the good word of how your APIs and other products can revolutionize, improve, and inspire how they perform their jobs.

But shouting your praises is only half of the equation. A good evangelism program not only spreads the word to your target audiences, it also carefully listens and reacts when they suggest improvements. Your evangelism efforts need to be a two-way street, not just impressing your customers with your abilities, but also forming meaningful relationships that raise everyone up at once.

Evangelist

Developer evangelist is a tough job that often requires quite a bit of travel and weekend work. Still, the right person will find that it brings satisfaction and opportunities unmatched by any other role.

Developer evangelists need to not only intimately understand the technology they're promoting, but also the other technologies target customers use and how to bring them together. The best developer evangelists can program in multiple languages, have an innate interest and knowledge of a broad swath of technologies that go well beyond their stated focus, and can jump in and help any developer with practically any problem they encounter.

But what sets a great developer evangelist apart from the rest of the pack is their ability to communicate with both developers and the business team in clear language that each audience can understand. They often act as the bridge between the technical and non-technical sides of their organization. When they're not evangelizing the value and ease of use of your APIs to customers, they're evangelizing your program's capabilities and advocating improvements to the rest of your company.

While "evangelist" is the title you most often see associated with this role, in recent years, I've grown more partial to the term "advocate." Where an evangelist is typically outward-facing, an advocate also works on behalf of customers to improve the experience and better address their needs. Whatever title you give this position, the role should act as a conduit between your technical customers and the teams that serve them. As a result, your developer evangelist may also act as your API product manager and vice versa.

Community manager

If your program is externally-facing and targeting the open developer ecosystem, assigning account managers to each developer who implements your API is all but impossible to scale. A better approach is to create and foster a community of developers around your product by providing a central location for them to find information and each other, and to communicate and create content and events designed to encourage their use of your services.

Your community manager is the person charged with setting the strategy for this community and helping to foster its growth. While this role can easily be filled by a developer evangelist, you may find it helpful to set this as its own role. Unlike an evangelist, the community manager doesn't necessarily need to have deep technical knowledge, but must instead understand how to bring people together and help them help each other. They should monitor the forums, chatrooms, and any other channels where developers gather to talk about their work for unanswered questions or negative feedback. They should also freely reach out with answers when they can, encourage positive feedback, and help build a real sense of community among your customers.

How big does this team need to be?

As I stated in the beginning, the roles listed above do not necessarily map directly to individual team members. In the early days of your program, you'll likely have a couple of people fill a vast majority of these roles in one way or another. For example, in an internal-facing program, your API product manager may take on the developer evangelist, product marketing manager, and technical writer roles. If you're building APIs to serve your channel partnership program, your existing channel partner team may also fill some of the marketing roles. And note that a larger team is not always better. I have seen successful long-term API teams that consisted of two people perform as well as teams with 50.

Final thoughts

Understanding how others have built their API programs and structured their support can provide a good amount of guidance on how to structure your own program. But copying another's program and strategy and hoping for the same success is a version of "cargo culting" that rarely provides positive results. You must take the time to intimately understand your target customer audiences and the value you can provide, while also succeeding against the goals of your organization. As you build your team, make sure each of these roles is either covered or intentionally considered unnecessary for your needs, and be sure to look internally for employees who understand your goals when staffing your program. Only by going through these exercises will you be able to confidently know what your team should look like for executing successfully against your API strategy.

CHAPTER 5

Building the Business Case

It's time to put everything you've learned so far to use and start to build out a business case for establishing an API program. But where do you start? How do you organize, collect, and communicate the value of an API program? And what types of metrics should be considered to demonstrate this value?

This chapter looks at these questions and provides guidelines on how you can develop a solid cost/benefit analysis to convey to various stakeholders, including your executive team, business units, and product or engineering managers. It will help you develop an initial framework to use to create a solid business case, along with examples of KPIs and metrics to include. We all agree there is value to APIs (or else this book wouldn't exist, and you wouldn't be reading it)—now we just need to prove it!

Align with business drivers

The value of APIs and an associated API program can be difficult to quantify. Organizations often talk in "feel-

87

good" terms such as "improved efficiency," "better reuse," and "reduced costs," but how do you put actual numbers against these generic statements? Where do you start, and what is the potential impact on revenue, costs, and the bottom line? Before you can answer these questions, you first need to understand the goals of the organization. What is the corporate strategy? Is the company in pure growth mode (a start-up), or is there a large focus on margins and earnings before interest, taxes, and amortization (EBITA)? Is your industry growing, shrinking, or staying flat? Who are your competitors, and what are they doing?

Understanding the drivers of your organization and industry as a whole, and subsequently of its executive leadership and management teams, is critical to determining where to start with an API program.

If the planning process and supporting materials do not align with these drivers, it won't matter what the numbers look like, and you will have a much harder time getting buy-in and project approval.

Planning tools and frameworks

With an understanding of the corporate goals and strategy, you can now consider business case justifications and look at how to identify the first API project. For the latter, it can be useful to start with something like the McKinsey & Company approach that defines a prioritization matrix focused on the "Strategic Attractiveness" and "Readiness to Execute" dimensions. See Figure 5.

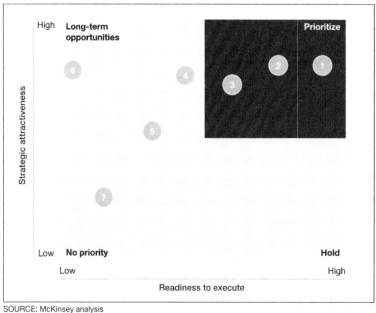

SOURCE: McKinsey analysis

McKinsey&Company

Figure 5. McKinsey & Company's prioritization matrix[3]

With this approach, API project opportunities are based on an analysis of the business impact, differential impact (vs. doing nothing), and contribution of APIs to company goals versus the technical difficulty and business, legal, and

---

[3] McKinsey and Company, What it really takes to capture the value of APIs, September 2017, https://mck.co/2L3Nc9Q.

policy readiness for building the APIs. The premise is that APIs that are strategic but very difficult to implement, or easy to build but have minimal business benefit, are likely not the best initial candidates for the API program. Find the right mix of business and technical benefits, along with the right supporting business sponsors, and you will have a much higher chance of success.

For the metrics themselves, you need to consider both the technical and business aspects of the program. Although I will present some specific considerations later in this chapter, in general, the business case should include any opportunities for monetization (see *Chapter 3:* for a deeper look at monetization strategies), the estimated business impact of the program (which may be supported by technical proof of concepts or prototypes), derived improvements in operational and technical efficiency, and any recommended organizational changes. Implementing APIs just because they are cool is not enough.

Drive the move towards using APIs within your organization with business requirements and the associated business value.

To collect this information and facilitate the development of underlying business case metrics and OKRs (objectives and key results), many approaches exist. Whether following a simple ROI calculator, an interactive spreadsheet, or more formal approaches, it is vital to use a method that is transparent, easy to follow, and simple to understand. Show how numbers were derived, list assumptions, and do not bury less favorable results in the fine print. Also note that the value of the program may differ across various areas of the business. One area may be focused on operational efficiency, while another on revenue generation. In these cases, it can be useful to have one section of the business case focused on the broader opportunity, with other sections providing details behind each supporting pillar.

One specific mechanism that can be valuable to study when developing your business case is the Business Model Canvas template,[4] commonly used for broader business contexts such as defining the business model behind a startup or an organization's products or services.

It may seem a bit odd to think of your API program as a business model. Still, there are some similarities between creating the API business case and describing a company's business value propositions. Some examples of using this approach in the context of APIs appear below. In many cases, merely going through the process and asking the questions can be valuable, even if the format is not a fit for your needs.

––––––––––––––––––––––––

[4] The Business Model Canvas: nine business model building blocks, Osterwalder, pigneur & al. 2010, https://bit.ly/3dlxovm.

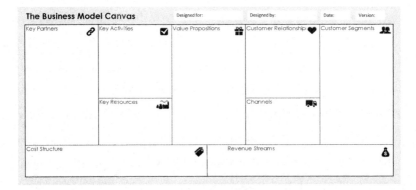

Figure 6 Business Model Canvas template (Reprinted by permission from Strategyzer AG. www.strategyzer.com)

Applying the Business Model Canvas to APIs

Area	API Context
Key Partners	This area would look at your API consumer audience from the perspective of key partners who could benefit from your API program or who you need to work with to deliver your API program. Who are the target partners for your APIs? What revenue opportunities are associated with these partners? What revenue opportunities may open up to your partners due to these APIs? Is there an opportunity to reduce acquisition costs via improved self-service capabilities and support? Will the APIs make your services "sticky" and streamline data exchanges with your partners? Are there opportunities to service more partners, or to provide better service to existing partners? Are your partners ready to participate in an API program?

Area	API Context
Key Activities	Key activities relate to the identified value propositions, and provide details on what to do to deliver the value. Establishing the API program is an obvious first step, but this category covers much more. How will the program be established, run, and supported? What type of marketing (internal or external) is needed to support the program?
Key Resources	Key resources are also typically related to the value propositions. What resources are needed to implement the API program successfully? Technical and business resources? What level of buy-in is required for the program to continue? Are there key resources required that are currently outside of the organization?
Value Propositions	This category covers the value that your API program will bring to the organization and the identified API consumers, including definitions of increased business functionality, improvements in revenue or costs, efficiency improvements, service delivery enhancements, and competitive differentiation. Use real numbers as much as possible when describing these items.
Customer Relationships	Customer relationships can include the onboarding of API consumers into your program, and the subsequent support they receive. How will you acquire these consumers? How will acquired consumers be supported? How will the list of consumers increase over time?

Area	API Context
Channels	In this context, channels are the mechanisms by which the APIs and the API program will be distributed to their users. Channels refer to both the technical assets and the end-to-end customer journey. How will the APIs be marketed? How will consumers be able to test or evaluate the APIs? How will purchases or access be provided? How will the program provide ongoing support?
Customer Segments	This area considers API consumers who are not key partners, including external or internal developers, either within your industry or across industries.
Cost Structure	Cost structure can refer to the costs of the API program, the costs associated with realizing the identified value propositions or revenue streams, and the costs of key resources and activities. An API program can result in new costs, but it obviously (and hopefully!) can also result in reduced costs in other areas. This section can also be useful for looking at the costs required over time and how they might evolve.
Revenue Streams	Revenue streams can deal with new sources of revenue, improvement to existing revenue sources, or the use of API monetization strategies. How will the API program impact revenue both inside and outside of the organization? What is the pricing model? Is there a charge-back model? Usage-based pricing?

Again, these are some examples, but the framework can be a handy way to organize and build your business case.

Key metrics and considerations

Now that you understand the broader problem and have established a framework for best representing the business case, let's cover some specific metrics and considerations. This is not an exhaustive list, but rather a starting point for your own program. Some of these factors will be more relevant than others, or you may have metrics and value propositions that are specific to your industry or organization. In the end, the result will be a set of considerations to support your business case and define what success looks like for you.

Business impact and strategic value

From a business standpoint, considerations such as the following are useful to include in your analysis. Be as specific as possible! It is not enough to say that APIs will "increase efficiency." What type of efficiency? In what part of the business? By how much? And how does that contribute to the organization's OKRs? Some of the numbers will be guesses, but they should be educated guesses with an associated set of verified assumptions and supporting materials.

⇒ *How will the API program improve the key business metrics identified in the company strategy? This may include considerations such as net promoter score (NPS), improved* customer recommendations/upsell, improved customer retention rates, and reduced customer acquisition costs (CAC).

⇒ What impact will the API program have on the average revenue per user (ARPU)? On the lifetime value of the customer (LTV)? For external or paid-access APIs, what is the monthly revenue or average contract value (ACV)? What is the percentage of users who refer new users to your APIs?

⇒ What new revenue opportunities would be enabled through the use of APIs? New monetization strategies? Would new channels or partners be possible, and what would be the associated uplift in revenue and profit?

⇒ How would the API program enable the organization to differentiate from its competitors? Is there an opportunity to gain revenue or market share from competitors and competitive offerings? Does this make the organization's products and services "stickier"?

⇒ What opportunities would the API program provide for increasing data security? Data sovereignty and self-service? Improving data quality and consistency, and streamlining data delivery?

⇒ How would the API program reduce the time to deliver new business capabilities? Change or support existing capabilities? Reduce errors due to mistakes in code or *supporting business logic? What would be the average reduction in time? And how does this translate to cost or revenue?*

⇒ *How would the API program support M&A activity? Or allow for the retirement of legacy applications? And support a move to a cloud-first strategy for the organization's applications, services, and data?*

Technical impact and alignment

The technical value of APIs can often be easier to justify, since the need for an API program is likely being driven largely by an IT-related group within the company. However, as with the business impact, it is important to be as specific as possible. Also remember that you need to consider the total cost of ownership over time, and not simply the costs or benefits associated with an initial implementation. You may be supporting these APIs for a very long time!

⇒ *What training requirements are needed for the staff to develop and support the program? What are the related software acquisition or subscription costs? Are new resources required? What are the associated consulting costs (if any)?*

⇒ *What organizational changes are needed to support the program, and what are the associated costs or expected efficiencies? Is a Center of Excellence (CoE) recommended? How will these changes align with the current business domains? Will API product owners be assigned to these business domains?*

⇒ *How will reuse be improved within the organization? What level of reuse can we expect? What will be the related improvements in cost, time to market, or revenue? How does this drive continuous innovation?*

⇒ *Will moving to APIs improve technical solution management and maintainability? How will support costs and response times be improved? What will be the expected impact to infrastructure costs? Will the organization's ability to diagnose and recover from issues be improved? What are the expected benefits in terms of response times to customer issues and system outages?*

⇒ *What is the expected improvement in developer productivity? What is the impact to the end-to-end development process? How can we improve code quality, testing, and production rollouts?*

⇒ *How can we improve the time and effort required to integrate systems due to M&A activity?*

⇒ *How can we reduce operating costs? How will the API program allow IT to shift further from being a cost center to a key partner of the business?*

Putting it together

You've done it! You have put together a set of business and technical justifications for your API program, supported these justifications with a strong set of numbers and assumptions, and wrapped this information into a nice package that is ready to share formally. If things have gone well, the final set of materials should not come as a surprise to anyone; the various stakeholders have been engaged throughout the process (*right*?), and all feedback has been incorporated.

One mistake that is common at this point is to share the material in the same format with everyone: executives, business unit owners, and product and engineering managers. Instead, to be more effective, the material should be structured to fit your audience. The executive team, for example, will likely be less interested in the technical details, while the business unit owners will focus on how the program will help their specific goals and objectives. Customize the materials to provide the right level of detail, and don't forget that not everyone will know what is meant by an "API"! Examples from everyday life can be handy in this case: the airline and ride-sharing industries are good places to start if this background and context is needed.

Lastly, it can also be useful to discuss how teams outside of the API program could be rewarded for API usage and for making improvement suggestions, and to discuss plans for how success stories will be shared across the organization. Enlist the assistance of "early adopters" within the organization, and remember that this process never stops.

The need to convey business value is ongoing, and a key element of the program's success. Keep improving, measure often, and don't be afraid to celebrate victories and learn from the failures.

Now that this part of the process is complete, you are ready to move forward. The real fun starts now!

CHAPTER 6

Understanding the Developer Audience

Developers have earned a reputation for being a rather finicky, contentious bunch. The stereotype is of a socially maladjusted nerd who locks himself (and it's always a *him*) in a darkened room to weave arcane magic from pure code.

Disavow yourself of these myths right now. Developers are as diverse and interesting a bunch that you're likely to come across, and their areas of expertise and interest span the entire spectrum of technology, from web applications to embedded technologies to genomic research and more. Many of these differences have caused internal battles within the larger developer community, which itself is loosely coupled and difficult to properly define.

It's critical to keep these differences in mind as you work to define the subcategories of developers who you believe would genuinely benefit from your API program. Even if you're targeting a mostly internal audience over which you think you have some control, don't overlook the necessity of evangelizing your program to them and keeping their needs in mind as you develop the details that support your program.

Three virtues of the programmer

With all this diversity in the developer community, it can be difficult to know where to start. Psychographics—understanding the mindset of your target audience—can be a helpful first step, but getting on the developer wavelength is often a challenge for the average non-technical marketer.

Larry Wall is a linguist who became an early free software and Internet hero when he created the Perl language, considered by many to be the "duct tape" of the early Internet. His sense of humor expressed in his writing, frequent technical talks, and even the comments in his source code, are completely in line with the off-the-wall and often anti-establishment attitudes of those early computing pioneers.

In his introduction to "Programming Perl," with its iconic "O'Reilly Zoo" illustration of a camel on its cover, Wall wrote that it was not his intent to teach the reader to program, but that ". . . the perceptive reader will pick up some of the art, and a little of the science, of programming. . . .We will encourage you to develop the three great virtues of a programmer: **laziness**, **impatience**, and **hubris**."

These virtues provide a helpful view into the mind of the typical developer.

Laziness

"The quality that makes you go to great effort to reduce overall energy expenditure. It makes you write labor-saving programs that other people will find useful, and then document what you wrote so you don't have to answer so many questions about it. Hence, the first great virtue of a programmer."[5]

It's a myth to call developers "lazy." As I've already pointed out, many of them are constantly busy and under pressure to deliver workable code. This translates, however, into a need to not do the same work twice, to find any short cut feasible, and to adopt practices that often rely heavily on the work of others. You see this in their use of common libraries, dictums that encourage DRY ("Don't Repeat Yourself") styles of coding, and even development tools that auto-complete as they type their code. This "laziness" actually improves efficiency and allows developers not only to get more done in less time,

---

[5] Quotes from "Programming Perl" glossary, 4th edition.

but also to rely on established code as a base to build new code in the hopes of limiting performance issues and bugs.

Impatience

"The anger you feel when the computer is being lazy. This makes you write programs that don't just react to your needs, but actually anticipate them. Or at least that pretend to. Hence, the second great virtue of a programmer."[6]

Computers are truly amazing machines, capable of handling thousands of insanely complex calculations in a matter of seconds. As they have become more powerful, the number of processes they can handle in a second has grown exponentially, following a curve that's become known as Moore's Law.

To a developer, though, computers are still too slow. With the constant pressure to get things done, every second can be felt, especially in the heat of developing something new or trying to fix an issue. Developers demand the most performance they can get out of any system and will loudly grumble at inefficiency. Likewise, they will do everything they can to speed things along and rapidly find alternatives if whatever they're relying on is slowing them down. This impatience frequently leads to lower latency,

---

[6] Quotes from "Programming Perl" glossary, 4th edition.

faster development processes, and new and interesting hacks that lead to better code.

Hubris

"Excessive pride, the sort of thing for which Zeus zaps you. Also the quality that makes you write (and maintain) programs that other people won't want to say bad things about. Hence, the third great virtue of a programmer."[7]

The best developers believe they can do anything with their code, which can make some programmers seem arrogant. I have never met a developer who didn't suffer from some amount of imposter syndrome, so I tend not to associate this with true arrogance and more with the pride and respect that comes from having so much knowledge and capability at one's fingertips. To quote another member of the geek pantheon, "With great power comes great responsibility."

Programming is one of the few disciplines where you can immediately put what you've newly learned to work and see direct results. I know several developers who have confidently said "yes" to some request without actually knowing how they might fulfill it solely because they

---

[7] Quotes from "Programming Perl" glossary, 4th edition.

know that, with enough time and resources, they'll figure it out.

That pride also encourages great programmers to do everything they can to make their programs something worth bragging about, whether another soul ever sees it or not. Even the most innocuous script—something no one but the programmer will likely ever see—is worth refining into an elegant piece of code that can hum along happily performing its job in a way that no one ever notices, but everyone relies upon. That sense of accomplishment is what drives many developers through their darkest hours of coding. The overwhelming feeling of joy that comes from figuring out a tricky bug or producing some piece of code that "just works", can erase much of the frustration and anger that led up to that point.

What all developers value (despite their differences)

The reputation that developers have earned of disliking marketing comes from the fact that most traditional marketing techniques rely quite a bit on broadcasting to a wide audience using clever imagery and messaging. This may appeal to the majority, but often doesn't directly address the specific challenges customers are seeking to solve.

Most developers know their subject matter intimately and are well-attuned to marketing content that doesn't get the details right. Developers are busy. They don't generally want to take the time to read your six-page whitepaper, sit through your non-technical 30-minute webinar, or act on your flashy advertising spread unless they see the clear value in what you're offering. If you can't quickly and clearly explain how your product solves one of a programmer's most challenging problems, they will pass on it without a second look.

More than that, though, developers tend to be extremely vocal about their preferences, and will readily share their experiences with their peers. If you stretch the truth, oversell your capabilities, or commit some error that negatively impacts a developer's ability to get their job done, you can be sure they'll be sharing that on blog posts, conference talks, developer forums, and social media. On the flip side, if your product clearly addresses developer needs, lives up to the promise of your marketing, and makes their lives easier, those same developers will sing your praises to anyone willing to listen.

Every aspect of your API program must clearly address the needs of the developer and appeal to the things they value. When it comes to your APIs, there are two values most developers put above all others: uniqueness of data and functionality, and reduction of developer effort.

If you provide a set of data or services that no one else offers or are difficult to replicate, the developers who need your services have little choice but to use your products. Proprietary data can be tremendously valuable and potentially give you a small, natural monopoly. But this can be a double-edged sword. Controlling a monopoly can be great for business, but it can lead to complacency, which can lead to a bad developer experience. If there's enough money to be made in the products you're selling, you likely won't be the only provider for long. Complacency in how you work with your developer customers leaves the door open for competitors who provide a better experience to come along and steal your business. Good interface design, documentation, and support is crucial even if you're the only game in town.

Products that reduce developer effort and provide a great experience win the crowd every time. Many of the early developer-focused products—tools like GitHub, code editors like IntelliJ, and infrastructure hosts like Heroku— were originally designed and built by developers to solve the problems they were seeing with existing products. In most cases, the improvements focused less on technological breakthroughs or better algorithms and more on providing an experience that helps developers become more effective. Many of these types of products have developed a cult-like following where users, who receive no remuneration from the companies, actively and passionately evangelize to their peers.

APIs that are easy to understand, easy to use, and easy to integrate not only keep developers coming back, but encourage them to share their experience with others, which can create a virtuous cycle that leads to success.

No one expects perfection out of the gate, and the developer audience can and will be very forgiving with early efforts that may fall flat, but only if you maintain a laser focus on addressing their needs and improving their ability to execute. For example, improving your documentation by moving difficult to search and read PDFs to easily searchable and scrollable HTML pages will likely win you praise. Changing the layout of the developer portal so it's more aligned with your corporate branding while your documentation is still a mess, however, will lose customers over time.

A multi-dimensional approach to developer segmentation

Though they have a lot in common, the overall developer community remains extremely diverse, not only in traditional demographic terms, but also in how they approach their work. Broadcasting to the wider developer audience and treating them as a homogenous group is a recipe for wasted time and effort on your part. It's not enough to "target developers" as an audience; you need to identify the key segments and subcategories to provide the most value. Saying you're targeting the developer segment, then producing hundreds of T-shirts with a Star Trek quote to hand out at your next conference, is a great way to clothe a bunch of people who will likely never buy your product.[8]

Audience segmentation is really more art than science, and that tends to be even more true of developers. Identifying the dimensions of segmentation can be tricky. You might first consider segmenting on items like programming language preference, operating system, or preferred cloud platform. The nature of APIs to be agnostic to many of these selections, however, means segmenting along these lines doesn't provide much guidance, at least in the beginning.

When going through this exercise with API program managers, you may want to focus on three key areas: the developer's relationship to the organization, their working environment, and the type of products on which they work. Each dimension unlocks several details that help

---

[8] Based on true stories.

shape the ideal customers and keep them informed of the other developer-focused products, marketing, and support offered.

You should consider these segments as you plan your own program, but don't stop there. How you differentiate your program from your competition will have a lot to do with how well you understand your developer segments and provide for their needs. There's no one-size-fits-all solution to this, but understanding whether and how you target these first three dimensions will help surface other qualities to which you should pay attention. You should revisit this exercise regularly, at least once a quarter, with the results being to update, iterate, and grow your approach as the market evolves.

Relationship to your organization

The developer's relationship to your organization can help determine what kinds of data and levels of access to provide, the levels of security and monitoring you need to put in place, how to provide support when they run into problems, and more. The importance of this segmentation becomes especially clear as you plan how to manage your APIs and select an API management system.

Citizen developers

It's difficult to think of any single industry that hasn't been radically changed by the advent of affordable computing and the Internet. Farmers rely on software to manage the planting, maintenance, and harvest of their crops. Mining companies use sophisticated data analysis to determine how productive a particular area may be and to scout for new locations. Beer breweries can all but completely automate the brewing process, reducing labor costs and ensuring a consistency in their product that was difficult before automation.

In the early days of personal computing, experts said computers were the new literacy. No industry and no job are left untouched by computers these days. If you look at the IT budget of any major company today, you'll find software purchases not only in the IT and engineering groups, but also in operations, marketing, finance, and sales.

But so much of that computational ability is restricted to only the functionality pre-programmed in the user interface. If you want to do something beyond what the interface allows, you'll typically need to do some programming.

For at least a decade, experts have said that programming is the new computer literacy, prompting the creation of dozens of coding boot camps, online schools, tutorial groups, and more. But learning a programming language is not exactly the same as learning to program, and knowing one well doesn't necessarily mean you know the other.

Programming is the art of using computer logic to design interactions and transform data into something useful. Full-time professional programmers are often asked to create interactions and transformations without deeply understanding the underlying data or the use cases. While a number of processes and development styles have emerged to address this—and many of them do it well—a lack of subject matter expertise can still lead to applications that don't quite live up to their purpose. Further, the IT and engineering organizations within most companies are so focused and overloaded on their core products and applications that small, one-off, internal projects that improve workplace efficiency, drive more customers, or add revenue, are often given a lower priority, if engineering or IT teams ever get a chance to tackle them at all.

Consider marketing and sales organizations. Interactive marketing experiences and demos that are not part of the main product have still proven to be valuable in driving new sales leads and opening a company to new markets. At one email marketing company, for example, executive leaders identified a need to provide non-technical small business owners who don't have the time or experience to learn HTML and CSS, the ability to create email templates that adhere to their website branding. The engineering roadmap was already tight with feature requests and enhancements that were deemed higher priority, which meant such a tool was placed on the back-burner.

Using APIs already exposed to allow customers and partners to better integrate with its system, the company designed and built a tool that took a website URL, extracted the main colors and images, and applied them to one of a set of several pre-designed email layouts. Non-technical users simply had to drop the URL into the tool to start designing an email template that fit their branding by clicking on the colors and images they wanted to add.

The trend of traditionally non-technical divisions hiring developers and more technically-minded staff has grown in recent years, and will only keep growing as the value of letting subject matter experts focus on building their own applications and interactions increases. Numerous marketing teams employ "marketing technologists" to integrate with tools like Salesforce to create custom reports and customer interactions based on the data flowing from those APIs.

The range of technical knowledge these developers have is difficult to pin down. Some are former full-time developers who have a strong interest in moving to the business side of the house. Others never held a programming job, but were drawn to development as a hobby or out of necessity.

The advent of low-code and no-code tools like IFTTT, Zapier, and TIBCO Cloud™ Live Apps has opened the ability for people who have never even considered writing a line of code to create programmatic interactions. In my opinion, this is the next step in computer literacy, not necessarily learning a programming language, but learning programming logic and applying it through an interface that is less restrictive than your average application. Empowering subject matter experts to create their own applications, whether internal-only or customer-facing, can significantly ramp up the productivity of your teams and give them greater control over the success of their careers. Targeting this audience can enhance your product's utility and longevity, letting you focus on satisfying a majority of your customers, while those with more esoteric needs can use your APIs to customize their experience and more intimately integrate your product with their systems.

These workers were dubbed "citizen developers" by Gartner, and they represent perhaps the most diverse of all of the developer personas. If this is an audience you intend to target, you should spend the time to narrow your focus by identifying the members most likely to leverage your APIs in this way. What is their department? For what organizational information and workflows are they responsible? How much technical knowledge do they have on average? What tools do they use with which you should integrate?

Because this audience, on average, has the least amount of technical knowledge, they will require an inordinate amount of guidance. To make this easier, you should create pre-built integrations with the tools they most commonly use that leverage your APIs. If they are using Salesforce to gather customer data that can be used with your systems, create and promote a connector for Salesforce. If they want to be able to mix your APIs with those of other major vendors, consider working with IFTTT or TIBCO Cloud™ Live Apps to create hosted connections through these platforms. You should also stay abreast of the number of tools coming to market that make visual flow-based programming much easier for this audience.

You might find that more traditional developers also go this route, especially as they strive to help their non-engineering colleagues become more effective. If you help your developer customers help their citizen developers, they will handle a great deal of the support themselves.

External developers

If you adopt any of the first three API monetization models mentioned in Chapter 3, you will be targeting developers with whom you may not have much of a formal relationship beyond their being a customer. In these cases, your APIs will be made available through a public portal with varying degrees of access based on how those customers use your services.

External developers can be existing customers of your application, consumers of your data products, or third-party affiliates who embed some of your data and functionality into their applications, but are otherwise not strategic partners. In all cases, maintaining tight control over who has access to what data is critical. API management tools that allow you to segment your services by binding access to user roles go a long way to making your APIs secure.

The size of the external audience is often directly related to your success in reaching out to developers and providing a great experience, which may make it your largest segment. If your goal is to build a third-party ecosystem with your APIs, you'll likely want to make at least some low-level access available to any developers who request access, perhaps even without anyone on your staff manually approving.

Allowing developers to onboard themselves automatically cuts a major barrier to developer adoption, but it may also reduce the return you see on your investments as lower-value customers consume as much or, in some cases, more resources than your high-value customers. This is especially true if you design your API to drive revenue-generating activities, such as selling tickets for travel or events. The computational power to query multiple backend systems for a search across a wide range of products is often greater than that required to actually book the sale. If you have an extremely high ratio of queries against a lower number of bookings (known as the "look-to-book" ratio in many industries), you may find the revenue from the bookings is not adequately covering your costs.

An even bigger concern is when you factor in the costs of supporting these developers when they run into problems.

A low-value developer today will never become a high-value customer tomorrow if they run into an issue with your product they can't resolve, so you need to strike a balance between providing detailed, intensive, hands-on support, and controlling costs.

You can address these issues by segmenting further based on the value of your customers, however your organization chooses to measure that value. Developers who are not producing much revenue or value for the API provider, either because they're just starting out or don't really have the audience, tend to understand when they run up against performance and access limits and don't receive concierge-level support. To help those who may eventually become high-value, however, you should put as much effort as possible into making both your onboarding and support processes completely self-service.

Though you should provide higher levels of performance and more personalized support to your high-value customers, they will also benefit from your efforts at providing a self-service experience. Automate as much as you can so that your personalized support efforts are focused more on addressing detailed or edge-case situations rather than answering basic questions.

As your external users grow and become more important to the success of your business, their sensitivity to technical issues and performance problems increases, especially if they find their own users and customers are experiencing problems. Decide the best way to communicate with your developers—email, social media, developer forums, your own developer portal, or some combination—and post any new releases, performance issues, or anything else that may affect them as quickly and consistently as possible. Your own internal processes should enforce broadcasting this to all channels you support.

Trusted partners

Not all developers outside your organization are the same. If your API program is focused primarily on enhancing your strategic partnerships, providing access to vendors, or identifying a segment of customers whose value prompts you to build a closer relationship, the levels of access, performance, and support you provide will likely be deeper than the general external audience. This includes not only what data and functionality you provide and how much can be accessed over a certain period, but also how much control they have over their own accounts and access to monitoring and reporting to help their business planning.

These trusted relationships tend to lead to stronger relationships, where contracts, mutual goals, and general rapport encourage good behavior and put less pressure on security controls. The return on investment in supporting these developers is typically much higher than average because your support efforts often directly pay off in the form of improved time to market and integrations more aligned with your business goals.

Trusted partners may have specific requirements that either segment them into smaller groups with a handful of members or require some level of personalized access. Selecting an API management system that lets you customize these options without releasing code will dramatically ease the burden of managing so many different types of accounts. You should also assign representatives to own these accounts and act as the first point of contact for your partners, to ensure the partnership remains aligned with your goals.

Because the success of your partners is so tied with your own success, you should provide them with a more personalized level of support. The effort you put into making your onboarding and support as self-service as possible for external developers will also save you time and money for your trusted developers. But the time-sensitivity of their issues will likely mean they will want to ask a specific question and receive a personal answer as quickly as possible to prevent any implementation delays.

The representatives assigned to handle these accounts shouldn't be required to also provide technical support, but you need to provide them with resources to whom they can point their customers when things go wrong. A dedicated partner team may have dedicated technical support staff who can address all but the toughest technical issues. But even smaller programs should at least provide some access to one or more internal developers who know your APIs intimately and can work with customers to address their issues.

Internal developers

It may seem strange to think of the developers you've hired as a targeted customer segment, especially when they're likely the same developers who built your APIs. But they are your most critical segment, especially when the intent of your API program is to improve your organization's IT processes. The biggest difference between the developers who work for you and everyone else is how much control you have over how they work and what they produce.

As the proverbial shoemaker's children often go shoeless, the developer experience for many internal organizations often goes ignored. Many teams rely on old, poorly maintained intranets to share documentation, often in Microsoft Word and PDF documents culled from the paperwork produced during the planning stages of the APIs. This negligence hampers the ability for your programmers to find the answers they need, makes it difficult to bring new hires up to speed, and negatively affects your ability to deliver.

Good API program managers will treat the developer experience for their own colleagues with the same care they show for their customers. Fostering a culture where the developers themselves are responsible for creating this experience can make it even more valuable, and much of what is produced can also be used for your external audience. Doing this successfully requires your engineering management teams to reinforce the importance of writing solid first-level documentation, creating good specs that become your API contracts, and to ensure that developers take the time and care to do all this as part of their regular workload. Developers may feel the pressure to skip much of this during periods of heavy work and tight deadlines, but disciplined teams will see the long-term value of this effort and ensure they stick to their processes.

It may also seem strange to require API gateways and management systems for APIs that may never be exposed outside the organization, but adding a level of control between the APIs and consumers can identify problems faster, help collect vital statistics on the health, performance, and success of the APIs, and make managing internal access far easier when developers eventually move into other positions, both inside and outside of the organization. Even features such as access throttling can help ensure the whole system is not brought down by one poor performing piece of code.

Their working environment

Developers are strongly influenced by the types of companies for which they work, as this affects how much flexibility they have over their work environment, the tools they can choose, the influence they have in purchasing, and more. Though there are many ways to split this up, I find using nomenclature similar to what is used to define these kinds of businesses is a good dividing line.

Enterprise

Large, well-established organizations that generate hundreds of millions of dollars or more tend to get that way in part by optimizing their IT processes. Reliability and consistency are often more important than adopting the latest and greatest technologies, which can lead to a certain rigidity and inflexibility when it comes to selecting development tools and environments. Many of these companies still manage legacy hardware and software that was considered top of the line when the company was founded, but are now comparatively old and slow. But that legacy technology continues to drive the business, generate revenue and keep things moving, and will likely stay in place until any of that changes.

Enterprise developers, as a result, tend to focus on a handful of trusted, reliable tools for most of their career, many of which may not be considered glamorous compared to more recently released products. Many of these tools are supplied by software companies that are themselves considered enterprises. This space, up until recently, was dominated by the likes of Microsoft, Oracle, and SAP, well-known names in the space with a long history that saw them ascend from scrappy startup to tech behemoth.

All of this focus on reliability tends to make enterprises and the developers who work for them rather risk-averse. Most enterprise developers research and play with the latest and greatest technologies, but few are eager to recommend adding new technologies to the stack until they've been proven to not have any negative impacts on performance and stability.

Keep this in mind as messaging is built around the APIs that target the enterprise audience. If you gain a reputation for APIs that are slow, return inconsistent data, or respond with a lot of errors, you'll struggle to get enterprise developers to adopt your services. Put systems and processes in place that increase performance and reliability, and degrade gracefully with clear errors and service level agreements when things do go wrong. Adhering to those SLAs is crucial. If you say a problem will take 24 hours to address, the fix better be ready within the time specified.

Enterprise customers may require that these SLAs be enforced in some kind of formal contract or end-user licensing agreement, which may require you to adapt your onboarding process to add a layer where the contract must be signed and approved by both parties before full access can be granted to your APIs. The process of getting that contract approved, however, may take anywhere from a few minutes to several weeks or even months, which may slow their time to integration. In these cases, either opening access to a sandbox or providing restricted access that is released at close of contract can ensure that the approval process happens in parallel with development, making it possible for your customers to go live shortly after negotiations are complete.

The amount of money generated by enterprises makes them less price-sensitive to solutions that produce desired results. Vendors selling to them can, therefore, typically charge higher prices without scaring buyers away. But the value for that money should be clear in all of your marketing and interactions, and should continue throughout the entire developer experience.

One troubling trend I've long seen in products targeting enterprises is a seeming lack of effort in providing even a decent user experience. So much enterprise software feels clunky and old compared to most consumer-targeted software. This is an area that leaves many of these vendors absolutely ripe for disruption, and we're slowly seeing that play out in the industry as smaller players emerge with systems as reliable as established competitors, but providing an experience that better suits their customers and makes them more efficient.

The same is absolutely true of your developer experience. Many established vendors who provide their services in XML-based API styles such as SOAP and XML-RPC are seeing new and established customers flock toward providers who have adopted API styles like REST that can be easier to use and quicker to consume. Stripe, for example, seemingly overnight became a major player in the payments space, putting tremendous pressure on established competitors like PayPal because it focused solely on making the experience of integrating its services as friendly to developers as possible. Don't skimp on the developer experience just because your customers may be used to something more complex and less polished.

Startup

I'm never sure exactly where to put the dividing line between a startup company and enterprise. Is it when they generate more than $500 million? Is it when they grow beyond 1,000 employees? Is it when they go public or get acquired?

For our purposes, the cutoff, while still poorly defined, has less to do with size and revenue and more with flexibility. At some point, a company gets too big for individuals to effectively collaborate directly with every other employee, which leads to tighter processes and restrictions, which can lead to less flexibility in how developers work. This is when companies begin to exhibit properties that make them act more like an enterprise than a startup, even those that claim to maintain a "startup culture."

Smaller companies focused on growth should constantly innovate to expand their presence in the market, solve more problems for a wider array of customers, and continue optimizing their products, processes, and technology to generate more revenue. Startups and the developers who work for them, therefore, tend to be more open to experimentation and adopt newer technologies quicker, either because the products may solve a tricky problem or because the company is building from scratch.

Reliability and performance are still critical to startup developers, but getting traction, finding product-market fit, and attracting and keeping customers remain their top priority. They can be forgiving if something goes wrong with your APIs once or twice, but don't count on a third chance.

Startup development teams do generally agree on a standard set of development tools, but the processes to introduce new tools are less rigid than enterprises, giving startup developers a fair amount of flexibility over how they do their jobs. Teams will likely flock to a new product that helps them get the desired results faster.

Though early-stage companies may be more price-sensitive, well-funded startups are often willing to pay well for solutions that have a clear positive impact on revenue. But they're just as likely to go with lower-cost or no-cost solutions that may carry more risk, such as some of those provided by the open source community.

You can lower any perceived risk in adopting your API program by ensuring you are consistently communicating with your customers if anything should go wrong. When things are running smoothly, solicit feedback and suggestions for improvement and feature requests to grow your relationship with your customers.

Independent

The best developers often have one or more side projects in addition to their main job. Perhaps they're trying to make some money on the side, or maybe they're helping out a community organization, or maybe they're just scratching a personal itch. Often, developers opt to work on a side project to gain exposure to some new language or tool to burnish their skills.

Thousands of developers work completely independently as freelancers and contractors, coders for hire who swoop in, save the day, and move on to the next crisis. The grind of finding work, managing their own motivation, and occasionally going through cash flow dry spells is considered by many in this cadre as the price of freedom, one they gladly pay.

This freedom enables independent developers to have almost complete control over the tools they select and the processes they adopt. While much of this may be influenced by the clients for whom they work, many companies rely on their independent developers to make the technology decisions, dictating desired outcomes rather than language and environmental preferences.

In the downtime between contracts, many independent developers will split their time between learning how to do things better and sharing their knowledge with their peers as a form of self-marketing. This makes them natural evangelists for the best products that enable them to do their jobs.

If they are purchasing tools for a client, they will pass that cost directly to them, making them as price-sensitive in those cases as the clients they represent. For their own tools, they tend to only pay for those that have absolute value to them. A penny spent that can't be reimbursed is a penny lost.

Often, they live and die by billable hours, so any time spent on learning a new technology that can't be billed to a client represents a liability. Solicit regular feedback from your independent customers and find ways to reduce their time to adoption. If you solve a problem for one of their clients, the chances are good they'll turn to you again when they get their next contract.

What they work on

As computer technology has spread and embedded itself in practically every industry, developers have become more specialized, covering specific areas of concern. Some developers are focused entirely on data analysis for large bodies of information. Others are focused on the needs of a particular industry. When we talk about API consumers, however, breaking them up by where they work is likely to inform the kinds of support you should provide and how best to create an experience that lets them quickly apply your product and get back to the core of their focus.

Backend

Most applications that run on desktops, mobile phones, and other connected devices traditionally follow some version of a paradigm called "client-server architecture." In this model, a program called a "client" that's on a local device—either a mobile application, an internet-enabled software program, or even the basic web browser— communicates with a sibling application that's across the network on another system, called the server. The client typically interacts with a human user in some way through a graphical interface, which we usually call the "frontend" of the application. Much of the processing and business logic is typically done on the server side of the application, "the backend."

Backend developers are typically less concerned with making an application attractive or user-friendly to non-developer audiences. Instead, they focus on making the application functional and on exposing data and services to allow the client application and front-end developers to focus on the user experience. Most backend applications do this by exposing their own sets of APIs.

Backend developers are the most likely to be both your greatest evangelists and your toughest critics. They tend to have a good understanding of what goes into developing

132 • API SUCCESS

and maintaining a set of APIs and will not be shy to share their opinions. Much of this stems from how much they rely on products like yours to accomplish their jobs. If your APIs are responsive, performant, and provide the right data in the right format at the right time, you will find them at the centerpiece of a number of applications. If something goes wrong with your API and this affects those applications, you can expect a lot of noise, especially from the backend programmers.

Many backend developers strive to cover the "full stack" of technology that controls their applications—the user interface, business logic, data storage, and infrastructure. As applications become more complex, however, it's difficult to stay on top of every aspect of these technologies. Many backend developers will focus on specific application stacks or frameworks so their knowledge of other pieces is not as deep.

To help backend developers get their jobs done quickly, you may consider offering software development kits (SDKs) to ease development. SDKs are libraries written in specific programming languages that encapsulate complex functionality in function calls that feel more native to a developer's chosen language. In other words, SDKs take web APIs that are typically language and environment agnostic and expose them in language and environment-specific ways to make it easier for developers to integrate.

SDKs, sample code, and documentation best practices appear in later chapters, including *Chapter 12*. For now, it's important to understand that backend developers tend to be a bit more technically demanding than other types of developers, so providing deep technical assistance early and often can help keep them moving forward. Listen to their feedback, but collect and analyze it from across all developers to look for patterns that indicate ways to improve your APIs and the overall experience. The most vocal developers don't necessarily represent your entire audience, so make sure you're measuring the importance of the feedback you get against the goals of your other developers as well as your organization.

Frontend

The ease you experience when using online applications is largely thanks to the efforts of front-end developers. The front end can be a thin client, such as a browser-based application, which offloads much of the computing required to a backend server while capturing user input and displaying results. Or it can be a thick client, like a mobile or desktop application, that handles at least some of the computing locally while relying on the backend for data storage, interconnectivity, and more compute-heavy tasks.

Many front-end coders are themselves, graphical designers who learned the skills to make their designs functional. Those who did not start as designers tend to learn good design principles simply through their experience turning static designs into interactive interfaces. In all cases, front end developers tend to be more sensitive to the user experience than average. Functionality matters, but usability and form almost matter more.

When it comes to web applications, most front-end coders are well versed in the trinity of browser-based languages, which include HTML, CSS[9], and JavaScript. Many front-end coders do strive to learn as much about the backend as possible to better understand the full application stack, but, on average, front end coders tend to be less focused on server-side technologies than backend programmers. As a result, they may require a bit more documentation and support on the underlying APIs than other developers who may be closer to this stack. Ensuring your documentation is clear, easily scannable, and thorough goes a long way with this audience.

For front-end mobile application developers, providing access to your APIs through SDKs that are designed for mobile platforms, such as Apple iPhone and Google Android phones, can really increase development speed

---

[9] HTML and CSS are not, strictly speaking, programming languages since they primarily define the layout of a web page and the styling applied to it without much programming logic, like for-loops, conditional statements, functions, or variables. But they encode certain rules and behaviors that, for our purposes, make them close enough.

and improve overall adoption. For web application developers, providing sample code using popular JavaScript frameworks, such as Angular or React, can help them rapidly get up to speed. You may even consider providing drop-and-go JavaScript snippets and widgets that these developers can cut and paste directly into their code with few if any edits, aside from changing user-specific parameters. Google Analytics, for example, allows a web developer to set up an analytic environment using their web application, then produce a custom chunk of JavaScript that can immediately be dropped in a web page, blog template, or in web application code, enabling anyone with even slight front-end knowledge to leverage statistics gathering and analysis tools.

Putting it together

These dimensions of segmentation are good places to start but not necessarily complete. You will still need to go through the exercise of identifying your ideal developer customers and digging into the details of how they work, what they need to accomplish, and how best to serve their needs. The segments in this chapter should act as guides as you create your developer personas and measure the success of your program against your needs.

Do not skip the exercise of identifying these personas, however, as they will inform every decision you make about the entire developer experience, from the design of your API interface to the structure of your documentation. As you put your API developer portal together, you should review its utility against these personas to ensure it is addressing their needs to the best of your knowledge. Once launched, solicit the feedback of your developer audiences and use that to iteratively improve every aspect of the experience. In the next chapters, we will often refer back to these segments and personas as we describe ways to create an experience that will attract and retain as wide a developer audience as possible.

CHAPTER 7

Creating a Great Developer Experience

In Chapter 6, one theme kept emerging: to best serve developers and help them get started as quickly as possible, get out of their way but be ready to respond quickly when something goes wrong. Communication is the most critical aspect of your developer experience. Different developers have different needs and preferences, and you should try to address as many as possible for each of your relevant audiences. Provide all of the information you can in an organized way and allow the developer to decide how to proceed.

The ideal developer experience is one in which they intuitively understand how to access and use your product with the least amount of effort. In this Utopia, network latency is predictable if it exists at all, servers run flawlessly, and any errors that do happen are caught, handled, and corrected before the developers even know there's a problem. Such a paradise is likely beyond the reach of mere mortals, but you can come close if you pay attention to the details, put processes in place to discover issues early, and communicate liberally with your developer audiences on their terms.

Creating a great developer experience (DX) involves every interaction developers have with your program, both directly and indirectly. DX covers the design of the APIs themselves and the format of the data returned, including all web sites and pages you create for supporting developers. It encompasses the documentation, code samples, compiled libraries, forums, marketing, registration experience—every aspect of your program that developers encounter.

To give you a better understanding of how to positively influence the process, this chapter covers the general process developers follow when evaluating new tools and software. It then dives into the centerpiece of your developer experience and the single source of truth for your API program: your developer portal. The chapter ends with some recommendations and best practices for building a true community of developers who can evangelize on your behalf while also helping each other out. It's tempting to think the recommendations in this chapter only apply to developers outside your organization. Why create a portal with thorough documentation for the same people who likely built your APIs? A great developer experience not only helps improve adoption of your APIs, but it also helps those adopting developers become more effective in their work.

This is as true for third party developers and trusted partners as it is for your own developers. You should build good documentation practices, support flows, and consistent communications into every piece of software you produce, even if the intended audience is your own developers. By doing so, you, too, can reap the benefits of a great developer experience and give your programmers more room to write great code.

The developer's buyer journey & workflow

To provide the best possible developer experience, you need to understand the entire workflow the typical developer follows when researching how to solve problems encountered on the path to deploying their solution. Even with the diversity of developer types and tools, this workflow is fairly consistent.

Research

When looking for new tools to use, whether it is an API, a code editing environment, or an automated testing tool, most developers start by asking their peers for recommendations. This kind of social proof is critical when you're working under intense pressure to deliver your code on time and don't have the time to do a full product search.

The average developer is likely to ask their co-workers and friends and, in parallel, solicit opinions from their favorite online forums or search engine. Armed with recommendations, they'll seek to find any obvious pros and cons for each possible solution and try to find the one that best fits their immediate needs.

We'll cover developer outreach and marketing in more detail in the next chapter, but the overall developer experience starts at this point in their research and has a significant influence on the outcome. If you gain a reputation for having a product that is difficult to work with, is slow, or poorly supported, you likely won't find yourself on the shortlist of possibilities. In many cases, it only takes one bad experience passionately explained by someone the developer trusts to knock you out of the running. This may seem unfair, especially if the issue experienced by the developer was unique to them, but this kind of input is necessary when making a fast decision.

If potential customers are being driven away by the publicization of a few bad incidents, you should take the time to address those incidents and work with the affected developers to come to a resolution. Don't demand they take down the bad press, and don't try to win them back as customers. Instead, your best bet is to reach out to them, listen to their complaints, and make some substantial changes in your program to address the issue going forward. Even if it's only a good faith band-aid for something that can't easily be addressed, most developers are understanding. After all, they know what it takes to maintain software, and many may retract or tone down their negativity if they feel your response is genuine.

Hands-on experience

In my experience, the best way for a programmer to learn new technology is to try using it to build something, break it in the process, then figure out how to fix it. No amount of documentation, textbooks, lectures, or videos can replace the experience gained by doing.

Once a developer has their shortlist of products to research, they'll want to get their hands dirty to figure out just how well the products live up to the hype and how easily they fit into existing development processes. Many APIs and software tools offer a free trial or a free tier for just this reason. Ideally, a developer should be able to register and start using the tool immediately, even if it's through a limited sandbox. If getting hands-on experience requires a sales call, a lengthy approval process, or any other barrier, there's a good chance the developer will move on to the next solution, even if it's not as good.

If you are selling or otherwise restricting access to your external APIs, you should offer a free tier of access to them with complete self-service registration to allow developers to evaluate your program. The only limitation on this tier should be the frequency of access. For example, you may allow up to 100,000 calls a day for your regular customers and a max of 20 concurrent connections. Your free tier may limit this to 1,000 calls a day and two concurrent connections. You should provide enough access to allow for adequate evaluation and even initial development, but not enough to support a production-ready application.

If you can't provide a free tier, consider building a parallel sandbox environment. A sandbox environment contains sample data and functionality that matches what one may find in the live systems, but has been sanitized or anonymized to make it only useful as an example and not for commercial purposes.

Supplying and supporting a sandbox environment, however, is often easier said than done. If your APIs are only providing data, and not performing any sort of create/update/delete operations, then your sandbox only needs to provide endpoints and data structures that mimic production, but with static, fake data. If your API does allow for data manipulation, you'll need to decide how to build a sandbox environment that best matches the behavior of your production environment without requiring too much maintenance on the part of your engineering team.

An ideal sandbox is one where every user has their own copy of the sample data and each can make allowed changes without impacting other developers. One common method for supporting this capability is to use virtualized or containerized environments. Still, you will have to consider the cost of supporting these environments, how long you'll allow access to them for evaluation, and how to discard environments no longer being used.

It's worth the effort to plan for this capability, however, as providing such sample tiers will not only lower the barrier to evaluating and selecting your products, but it will also allow smoother subsequent development. Developers can use the free tier or sandbox to start their initial development using your APIs, and to later support any changes or upgrades they may make without impacting their live applications.

Selection and purchasing

Most developers have a great deal of flexibility and influence in selecting the tools they use, especially if no money is exchanging hands and no contracts need to be signed. Yet, they are rarely the ones who make the purchase. If your API requires no money to change hands and little more than a click-through end-user licensing agreement, then the developer is more likely to be the final

144 • API SUCCESS

decision-maker and will proceed with integrating your APIs in their project.

Anything further will require the involvement of their management teams and, likely, their legal and procurement processes. None of this should deter you from trying to directly monetize your APIs, but it does emphasize the need to ensure the process is worth the headache. If your competitors are not charging for similar functionality and data, you will need to demonstrate why your APIs are worth the hassle.

And, from a developer point of view, this purchase process is typically a hassle. Each organization handles procurement differently. Smaller companies usually move faster with little time spent on negotiation. Larger companies with full-time procurement teams are likely to carefully go over every line in the contract and negotiate hard on things like price, service-level agreements, and some things you may consider "nit-picky." This can be frustrating for developers because this timeline often slows their process. If you've provided a free tier or a sandbox, they can typically use that to work on their project during the contract negotiation, either flipping to a production account or changing the API key at deployment.

If the process takes longer and holds up any part of the project, the developer may work on something else while everything settles. Once it does settle, it can take the developer some time to get back into the rhythm of working with your APIs.

For the developer, this is all friction. If your APIs require this level of effort, make sure you reinforce the value of what the developer is getting at every stage of the purchase process. Give the developer the ammunition they need to properly recommend your products to management, then do everything you can to streamline the sales process and help the developer get up and running quickly.

Implementation and testing

Many developers will use the evaluation period to begin applying your APIs to their project, but their focus at first will be less on writing perfect code and more on ensuring you're solving their needs. Once they have selected your APIs as the solution, real implementation begins in earnest.

Implementation is where the rubber meets the road, and where the developer finds out just how effective a job they did during the evaluation phase. It can be incredibly frustrating to get so far with a solution, then find out there are details that only emerge under certain conditions that make the entire project unsustainable. This actually happens more often than you might expect. It can be incredibly inconvenient, but it's almost never too late to abandon a solution in favor of another.

How you react to developer needs during their implementation and testing phases may be the most critical aspect of your developer experience. If your API is well designed and intuitive, your documentation thorough and easy to search, and your sample code and tutorials comprehensive, most implementations will be a breeze. When things go off the rails (and they will), you'll need well-informed humans to jump in and help developers directly. This is where the developer experience most often falls apart for many programs.

A developer may reach out for more personalized support for a variety of reasons. In my experience, most developers prefer to find answers on their own because it's typically faster. But many developers in their haste will miss answers you consider as obvious in your documentation and will reach out to you directly. In this case, if more than 15% of developers reach out to you directly, it may indicate your documentation needs improving.

Some developers, however, just want to know there's a human on the other end of the line who can help them when things get sticky. For your high-value customers, make sure you have a process to quickly and directly address support questions as they arise, responding within hours rather than days. The faster you can help them, the faster they can complete their project, and the happier they will be in the long term. If you've built enough of an audience, you may be able to host a forum where developers can post their questions and receive answers from both other developers and your own staff. But no matter how you choose to accept support requests—in forums, by email, by phone, or through a ticketing system—be sure to respond as quickly as possible, even if it's just to say that someone is looking into the issue.

If a developer uncovers an error or limitation in your API that prevents them from moving forward, address it as quickly as possible. If you can't roll out a fix within a reasonable time, try to find a workaround that can suit the developer until you do. The goal is to help them get their project completed using your tools, tying your success to their success.

Deployment and maintenance

Once the developer has completed their work, they'll run it through final testing to make sure their code doesn't break anything in the system, then push it live once everything passes. If they developed against a limited or sandbox version of your APIs, this is when they'll need to switch their code to point to your production endpoints and use a production key.

In most cases, you'll have already provided the information they need to begin using your production services during the time you approved them as a developer. In rare cases, you may require an additional review of their application before providing access to your production capabilities.

Be careful about implementing this requirement, as doing so will add to your team's workload and will slow your customers' development time. In most cases, a pre-launch review won't uncover much. Instead, it's better to put limits on how many calls they can make per minute or per day, which should be high enough to use your system as intended, but catch unexpected floods of traffic before they impact other users.

Once a project is live, its continued success will depend largely on your services, even if you don't necessarily have direct access to the end-users. Your infrastructure must remain performant and accessible. Any outage in your APIs won't just affect your customers, but also the customers of your customers. Even if you can promise 99.9999…% uptime, you need to plan ahead for when things go wrong. Your system should degrade gracefully by providing meaningful errors to your developers' applications. Your documentation should also explain how developers should handle those errors in their code. Should they retry the call? Should they show an error to their users? Should they contact your support desk?

You should monitor all your APIs and their supporting systems and alert your team when anything happens that could impact users. If certain subsystems are consistently returning errors, timing out, or taking longer than expected to respond, it's better to have an automated alert sent to your on-duty support teams rather than field dozens of customer calls.

Similarly, your developer customers should be alerted whenever there's a possibility your services are affecting their code, so they can handle their own support queues effectively. You can leverage the same tools you use to monitor your services to provide a health check page that shows what services are working as expected and which ones may have problems. This level of transparency can be scary, especially if you're experiencing consistent issues that are difficult to fix. But a health page that shows your services in the "green" for long periods is also a potential piece of marketing collateral.

Build trust with your developers through honest and consistent communication and they will reward you with loyalty.

Inevitably, you'll need to make a change to your APIs that breaks the expectations of your developers and, thus, breaks their code. Chapter 10 covers versioning strategies—but the most important part of any versioning strategy is ensuring you communicate the changes that may impact developers early and give them the appropriate amount of time to apply and test changes before switching them to the new version.

Keeping the lines of communication open

Wherever the developers using your APIs are in their workflow, your most important role is to provide timely, consistent, and clear communication to quickly answer their questions, address their problems, and keep them productive. Your entire developer experience, from design to portal to documentation to marketing to support, should be built around communication as a priority.

But how much communication do you need? Too much, and you start annoying your developer customers almost as much as if you're providing too little.

The answer is that it's always better to communicate too often rather than not enough, and to allow developers to determine for themselves what they receive. Create as many communication channels as makes sense and let developers choose which ones they prefer. So long as each channel contains or points to the same information, and it's clear to developers which channels are available to them, you'll be able to share information effectively without putting too many people off.

Your dedicated developer portal

The one channel every developer should be required to visit is your central developer portal. The portal should be a developer-centric website, preferably hosted on your own domain with its own subdomain (for example, http://developer.example.com in Figure 7).

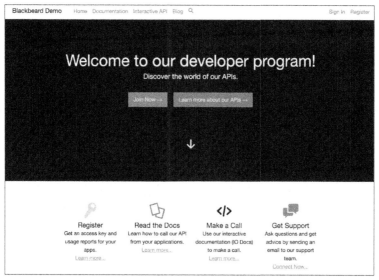

Figure 7. Developer portal

Your developer portal should be the single source of truth for everything regarding your APIs, and nothing else. Developers should not have to wade through your generic marketing materials, product configuration manuals, or support knowledgebase to get to the information they need. The portal is a hub that guides developers directly to the information they need with the least amount of friction. It will also likely host your API's registration forms, documentation, support forums, and developer tools. If any of those items are served elsewhere, the developer portal should at least make it easy to navigate to them.

The portal is also an opportunity to market to developers, but in a targeted fashion that considers their unique interests. During the evaluation stage, most developers will pore through your documentation, sample code, tutorials, and more to ensure your APIs will solve their challenges before writing a line of code. Existing developers will go through the same process when they expand their usage of your services or change their code to adapt to newly provided features and functionality.

The chances are good that your marketing team manages all of your websites and web assets. While the same team who runs your corporate website may also set up and manage the structure for your developer portal, your content, including any targeted marketing content, should come from the programmers that build your APIs, API product managers, and developer evangelists. A professional technical writer is also a good investment because most developers, though they know the technology intimately, are not the best at writing about it.

Thorough, searchable documentation

If your portal does nothing else, it must provide the best documentation available for your services. Good documentation significantly reduces development time and effort by providing clear and well-organized information appropriate for every developer's skill level and needs.

Figure 8. Sample documentation

Since different developers have different preferences, you should strive to address all of them, but leave it to them to decide which paths they wish to follow. For example, mature developers may not appreciate a page dedicated to how OAuth 2.0 is implemented, but novice developers may find it helpful as they try to access your APIs for the first time. Offering this type of information in a separate static webpage linked in the table of contents will allow those who want that information to find it and others to skip it.

Note that API documentation comes in two general forms, static and interactive. Each addresses different developer needs but works together to create a complete experience.

Static documentation

The vast majority of documentation you provide will likely be in the form of long-form manuals, webpages, and tutorials. This type of documentation should be static in the sense that it's straight text, diagrams, and code samples without any interactive features. But just because it is static doesn't mean that it is not changed. Update this documentation as your APIs change and allow your developers to provide feedback on how to make it more readable and useful. Treat all technical documentation as living documents that change as the code they describe changes.

Static documentation should be hosted directly on a website using basic HTML, CSS, and JavaScript rather than in long, difficult to scan and search PDFs or Word files. This lets readers use the robust features of their browser to scan, scroll, and search for the answers to their questions. It also allows for better search engine optimization, meaning your documentation should be listed when developers query their favorite search engine for answers.

Ideally, your static documentation should cover the most common and expected use cases and workflows your APIs were designed to address. It's likely your APIs aren't suitable for a linear narrative manual that flows easily from chapter to chapter. Instead, organize your documentation with chapter headings and links that drive developers directly to the problems they're trying to solve. For example, an e-commerce API may have a page describing how to implement authentication, another for how to browse products and add them to a shopping cart, then another that describes the checkout and payment processes. Each of these may call several API endpoints, but the documentation should describe the order in which to call them and how to use the data received from each to call the next.

Your static documentation should also describe decisions you have made in your API design that may not at first be intuitive to developers. For example, you may list the types of errors your API returns and describe how a developer can handle them. Whether you are following a commonly seen pattern or a best practice that is just gaining traction, you should describe how you have applied that functionality in your APIs, and how you expect developers to use them to avoid confusion.

One thing static documentation should not be used for, unless you have no other option, is as a service directory, a listing of every endpoint and every parameter the endpoint accepts. While these are necessary bodies of information, posting them in static web pages makes them difficult to read and search. I have never seen a service directory of this type that was clean and easy to read. It's better to provide this kind of information using an interactive format.

Interactive documentation

Thanks to the Open API Spec (OAS, aka Swagger), developers consuming web services are often blessed with the ability to try calls directly from their browser without writing a line of code. The OAS allows API providers to document every aspect of their API—endpoints, request and response parameters, URLs, common data objects, and more. Using a variety of tools, convert APIs that follow this spec into a set of interactive webpages that allow developers to make calls directly from their browser and immediately see the results.

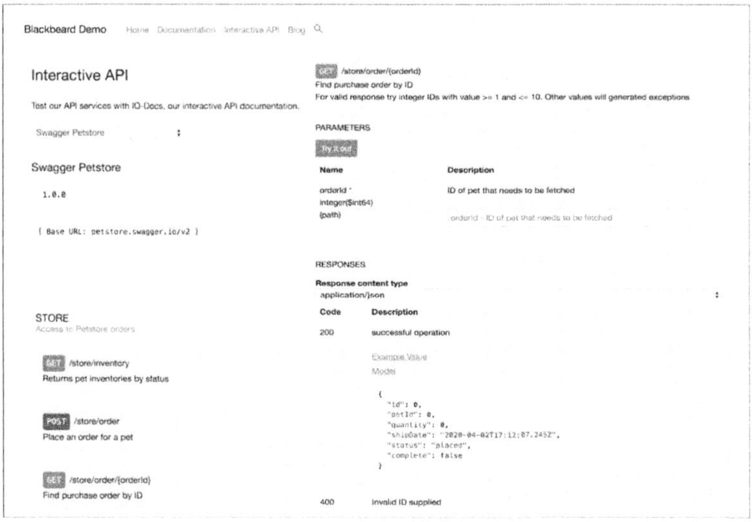

Figure 9. Interactive API

These pages are key for early-stage development in which a programmer is determining what is possible with the API. The pages act not only as documentation—a better form of detailed API description than the traditional service dictionary—but also as a prototyping tool. Some developers may even cut and paste the calls directly from these pages to form the basis of their application.

The OAS is not the only format available for this kind of documentation. There are several descriptor languages and formats from which to choose to help you design, document, and track your APIs, including RAML, Blueprint, IO Docs, and more. Some API styles may even have their own standard descriptor format, such as the WSDL often provided with a SOAP API.

Unless you are required for some reason to do otherwise, and if you are looking at traditional APIs based on REST, I strongly recommend adopting the latest version of the Open API Spec. At this writing, the OAS has emerged as the clear winner in the descriptor wars and has been adopted by most major API providers and vendors. In addition to providing interactive documentation out of the box, the OAS can act as the single source of truth describing how each of your endpoints is expected to operate.

This same documentation can be used to dynamically generate software client libraries customized to your APIs, inform automated testing and integration tools on the expected functionality of your endpoints, and even allow your developers to rapidly create fake API endpoints (mock APIs) for testing and validation purposes without writing much if any code themselves.

The world of APIs is constantly changing, and there may very well be newer, more widely adopted descriptor formats in the future. As with selecting the right format for your APIs, you should consider all of the costs and benefits of adopting a descriptor language before you commit. Once you have made your selection, you should be willing to provide the descriptions for each of your API endpoints to your developer customers, preferably on a resource-by-resource basis. This will allow them to use the most up to date version of your descriptors in their own tests and save time by automatically generating boilerplate code.

Clear path to registration

The simplest registration process is one that requires no intervention from your team, allows your developer customer to sign up themselves, requires no additional validation, and provides an API key immediately. However, no matter what the process, be sure to explain it thoroughly, even if only by using a simple diagram. Surprise endings and mysteries can be great, but not as part of your API registration process.

Figure 10. Registration

APIs containing sensitive data, especially those targeted to strategic partners and internal developers, will likely require some kind of human-led validation process before registration can be completed. Describe in detail the requirements developers must meet to register, the information they must provide, and what the approval process entails. Most importantly, communicate clearly how long they should expect to wait for approval and how the approval decision will be communicated to them. Most approvals shouldn't take more than one or two business days, and developers should be informed by email. If your approval process takes more than five business days, you should consider providing either limited temporary access or a sandbox so they may begin development while they wait.

Keep in mind that any delay in providing access will slow their process. If the developers can plan for these delays in advance, all the better. If you can't respond in the expected time, it will negatively impact their work. Communicate at every step, be clear about where they are in the process, and specify when they can expect a definitive answer.

Clear path to support

When a developer gets stuck working with your APIs, they will hopefully turn first to your documentation. If they don't find the answers there, they will look for whatever support you provide, such as an email address, phone number, forum, FAQ, or support ticket system. Failing that, they will turn to programming community sites like Stack Overflow to see if anyone else has run into a similar issue and found a solution.

Good documentation that is regularly updated to cover the most commonly reported issues will address the vast majority of support requests before they're even filed. Still, developers will find interesting edge cases and unique uses that will require the intervention of someone with more expert knowledge.

The first line of support after your documentation should be a website, email address, or phone number monitored by someone on your staff who can address developer-specific support issues and even walk through the code themselves. Be clear on your support level agreements and support them faithfully.

Even with a support line, many developers will turn to the communities they trust to find answers. You may provide your own set of forums for developers, but if they are not well monitored and regularly populated, most will skip them entirely and go to sites like Stack Overflow. Stack Overflow gets a lot of love in the developer community because of its searchability and how willing its members are to provide reliable help. In most cases, the issue for which someone is searching has already been addressed, so it's a matter of reading and applying the response.

Your support staff should be monitoring Stack Overflow and any other similar sites that you know your audience uses. They should actively and publicly answer any questions specific to your APIs and applications while also trying to follow up with more personal support if the situation warrants.

Building a community of developers

As adoption of your APIs gathers steam, you may find your developer audience beginning to communicate with one another through popular third-party communities such as Stack Overflow, Medium, or Hacker Noon. When solving difficult problems, developers tend to turn to their peers for advice and recommendations. Many share their own solutions to aid others in their search as a means of giving back to the community. Developers are inherently social and frequently use code developed by others in their projects.

You can improve the experience of your developer customers by fostering this communication and making it easier for them to help each other. There is also, of course, a marketing aspect to this. By building a community, you are building a relationship between your team and your customers, but that should be a secondary concern. Focus on creating a community that is active, helpful, and at least a little fun, and the marketing will all but take care of itself.

Online forums

In its simplest form, an active developer community can be as simple as a dedicated area for developers to ask questions and exchange information, and where your own team can quickly provide answers and join in the conversation. Whether hosted on your own developer portal site or a third-party site such as Reddit, the primary focus should be on providing support for your APIs and helping your customers.

In especially active forums, it's not uncommon to find certain members interacting closely with one another and creating genuine friendships. If the topics stray too far from your primary products, you may consider opening a separate area just for those off-topic discussions. Regardless, you will want to closely monitor these forums to ensure members remain civil to one another and be sure to jump in when discussions go too far off the rails. It's also common for online forums to become targets for unsolicited business posts (spam). Too many of these can make a forum look like it's only populated by scammy robots, which will drive active members away.

Meetups

To create deeper connections among your developer customers, as well as between them and your team, you may consider hosting live, in-person events near where many of your developers are located. Such meetups are very popular among technical professionals and offer an opportunity to meet others, do a little professional networking, and pick up some new skills and information, often while sipping a beer and chewing on some good food.

In the early days of your API, you may not have enough traction in any one geographic area to support such a meetup on your own. Typically, you need at least 100 individuals in a roughly 20-mile radius to attract enough people (at least 10) for a meetup to be worthwhile. But, every night meetups are hosted around the world, focused on more general areas organized by industry, specific programming languages and environments, areas of interest such as AI and machine learning, and even just for APIs and API programs in general. You should start by looking at the meetups that your staff can attend, ensure they're open to new members, and start attending them to network and get a feel for what the community is interested in hearing about. Attending these meetups can give your team a great idea of what developers are actively doing and concerned about, which can inform ways to improve your products.

Most meetups have a pretty standard agenda. Doors open early to allow for people to gather, grab some food and drink, and talk informally amongst themselves for 30 minutes to an hour. The guests are then asked to sit and listen to one or more speakers who will each talk for 20-45 minutes, then open the floor for an interactive Q&A. The organizer thanks all for coming, tees up excitement by explaining what will happen at the next meetup, then allows for another 30-60 minutes of networking before ending the event.

With so many meetups needing speakers, there's a tremendous opportunity for your team to find opportunities to talk before an eager crowd filled with members of your target audience. This is not the time for a sales pitch. Encourage your internal developers to share their experiences and knowledge with these groups to raise awareness of your organization and boost the profile of your developers within the community.

Social media

Social media platforms like Twitter, YouTube, and LinkedIn are an often-overlooked way to keep in contact with your developer audience and provide another avenue for continued support. Even if you already have a presence on most social media sites, you should create an additional targeted presence and promote this on your portal, forums, and in any other communication with your developer customers.

Not all platforms, however, are suitable for interacting with developers. Each one tends to operate for specific purposes. But there are a few you should consider:

- **Twitter**. Twitter messages must be no more than 280 characters long. That makes this technology ideal for short, to-the-point messages between users. Many developers will use Twitter to ask for help in the hope of reaching a live person who can provide personalized attention. Aside from direct messages, however, all Twitter communication is public. Your team should respond to Twitter requests and mentions appropriately and offer to take the conversation to a more controlled and targeted format such as email, Slack, or Gitter when necessary.

- **YouTube**. The popularity of Internet video continues to increase, with a surprisingly large community of developers turning directly to YouTube to learn new skills and find answers to their problems. The comments section is notorious for going wildly off-topic and occasionally inviting the more toxic elements to voice their opinions. Still, most users recognize all that as par for the course. A well-maintained YouTube channel containing videos that walk your customers through various features and how-to's for implementing your APIs can dramatically help improve your rate of adoption.

- **LinkedIn**. As you evaluate the social media platforms on which you should be active, consider what the average user thinks of them. LinkedIn, for example, is a popular platform across a wide set of demographics. However, it may not be the first place a developer turns to connect with you. Rely on feedback from your audience to determine whether to pursue LinkedIn and similar platforms as part of your social media strategy.

- **GitHub**. You may be surprised to find GitHub, a site that hosts online repositories for developers to track, version, and share their code with their teams, mentioned as a social media platform, but it has all the hallmarks. Users may share code snippets, comment on each other's code, submit fixes and features to improve hosted code, and otherwise socialize and communicate with one another. Any sample code, SDKs, or open source tools you provide should be hosted on GitHub and actively managed by members of your team. Users can submit bug reports and feature requests through GitHub's interface. They can also submit their own fixes and feature enhancements for your approval and inclusion in your code, though your own team should continue to do the same. GitHub is a great way to build an audience around specific pieces of code and create a collaborative development community.

Building a strong community not only helps your existing developer customers stay effective as they use your APIs, but it also demonstrates to prospective customers how strong your commitment is to your product and provides social proof that will encourage others to adopt your product.

Final thoughts

A great developer experience is ultimately the best arrow in your developer marketing quiver, keeping existing developers happy while attracting new ones to adopt your products. As with many organizations that target consumers, creating this experience for your developer audience involves many approaches and techniques, with no "one-size-fits-all" strategy. Look at your identified developer segments and personas, listen to their feedback and continuously evolve the experience as your program and customers mature. Finally, don't forget to put yourself in their shoes! After all, if you are having a great experience creating your API program, chances are that many of the same techniques can be adapted to do the same for your customers.

CHAPTER 8

Developer Evangelism, Advocacy, and Marketing

This chapter discusses how to reach developers and drive them to your API program. I present marketing methods that will be familiar to most marketers, only to show how they differ when targeting developers. Marketing your API program is not just about driving adoption to generate revenue, but it's also about helping to make developers successful. Developers hate being marketed to because so little of it exhibits enough understanding to be relevant. My goal is to show you how to do it right.

Practical problem solvers

To be a professional programmer is to be an expert problem solver. The ability to understand and solve complex problems with code is what ultimately separates the best developers from the rest of the pack.

> *It may sound obvious, but most developers don't really start looking for or paying attention to a solution until they have a clear problem to solve. This is one of the fundamental ways that marketing to developers differs from marketing to business and consumer customers.*

Quite a bit of traditional marketing—print advertisements, commercials, and pay-per-click ads—tries to convince customers they have to address a problem before they realize they have one. Developers tend to be so focused on their current projects that they put aside technologies for which they don't see a clear, immediate use.

This is not to say that traditional marketing and outreach activities don't work for developers, it just means your hit rate may be lower. If your entire marketing strategy relies solely on a developer remembering you when they eventually find a use for your product, you'll find yourself competing heavily against all the different tech vying for their attention.

Success relies heavily on building awareness of your products and capitalizing quickly when a developer's needs align with your solutions.

> *Building trust at every stage is critical because too many developers have been burned by products that over promised and under delivered.*

Far from a minor annoyance, adopting a technology that does not live up to its hype can completely devastate a software project and cause long-term effects that could require a complete rewrite from the ground up. One need only to experience this once to cast a skeptical eye on vendor marketing.

The right marketing strategy, therefore, must leverage traditional marketing methods and hands-on demonstrations of your APIs that prove and deliver on the promise.

Developer evangelism

The technical or developer evangelist role, introduced in *Chapter 4, Staffing Your API Program*, has become popular in the last few years as a way to address the unique challenges of marketing to a technical audience. The term "evangelism" should invoke some sense of dedication to a cause that compels one to share knowledge and experience with others. In other words, evangelism is an intense form of personalized marketing that has proven its value for expert audiences.

A developer evangelist is a person who not only intimately understands the product they represent and the audiences they are targeting, but can also get deep into the weeds with them. The best developer evangelists are developers themselves and know first-hand the development lifecycle and the challenges it creates.

Your developer evangelism team, which may at first consist of a single soul, should be your front line in every interaction you have with your developer audiences. They should sign off and have deep influence over every aspect of your developer experience, even if they're not directly responsible for creating the APIs. They should regularly contribute to your API documentation, tutorials, and marketing materials as well as attend developer-focused events as participants, mentors, and speakers. They should also contribute their own code to help make the lives of your developer customers easier and should continue sharpening their own skills to stay abreast of what's new in the industry.

Building trust with your developer customers is critical, and your developer evangelists play a key role. Customers should not view them as corporate marketing shills—they can't simply be parroting your marketing message and nothing else. Your evangelists should be free to address any technical questions or needs of your customers, and not just those related to your APIs and products. They should be allowed to be honest about the weaknesses of your program, though be ready to provide adequate workarounds and solutions. While it should be clear that they represent your company and strive to present it in the best possible light, they should put equal focus on building a meaningful rapport with developers who will then come to trust they will get reliable answers or be guided in a productive direction.

Finding the right person to be your developer evangelist can be tricky. Solid programming skills and experience are vital for the role, but solid communication skills are at least as important. Developers do not have a reputation for being great communicators, but many see the value in learning how to better share their ideas with their peers to move forward in their careers.

Most developers are evangelists for the things they love, so it's often more a matter of corralling this energy and excitement in a productive way to make them more effective.

The right candidate is someone who can speak to developers with ease, read and produce solid code, and comfortably write for and speak to large developer audiences. When they are not on the road attending and speaking at conferences or representing your program at hackathons, they should be shoring up your documentation, helping craft and review your developer messaging, and providing individualized support for your most valuable developer customers.

Chances are good the ideal evangelist candidate is already on your software engineering team. In the early days of your program, identify the individuals who have an interest in developing their communication skills or already proven them, and task them with the role of part-time evangelist. In some cases, the right person may be the product manager in charge of your APIs. If your APIs are mostly internally facing, every engineer who writes associated code should eventually become an internal evangelist in their own right. However, it's still critical to designate one or more people as the primary internal evangelist to address your team's questions and help them smoothly implement your APIs.

Developer advocacy

Where your developer evangelist fits into the organizational structure is a point of some debate within many organizations. It seems at first that the primary role of an evangelist is to perform specialized marketing, and thus many developer evangelists roll up into the marketing organization. But the most effective evangelists are those who are equal parts marketer and developer advocate.

Where evangelism is focused mostly on spreading the message of the company to its target audiences, advocacy focuses on making sure the organization remains responsive to the needs of their customers. A developer evangelist should, therefore, not only be concerned with making sure developers understand how to use the APIs and technologies, but they should also listen to developer concerns, pay attention to their struggles, and organize and share that information with the rest of the organization to inform and improve the overall developer experience.

Evangelists who work directly with customers and prospects on a regular basis are tremendously valuable sources of information when it comes to improving your products and identifying new markets and challenges to address. You must ensure there's a direct line of communication between your developer evangelists and your product management and marketing teams.

The importance of this role in a successful API program can't be overstated. Because of its importance, many have eschewed the title "developer evangelist" in favor of "developer advocate," with the tacit understanding that an advocate will still heavily evangelize your products.

The department the role belongs to is more or less irrelevant. The marketing team typically covers the costs of travel, sponsoring events, and producing content, so it may make sense to host the role with that team. Regardless of where your evangelists are based, they need to be comfortable collaborating with just about every department, including marketing, product management, software engineering, and even sales. They should act not only as the mouthpiece of your organization, but also as a conduit for developers to inform the evolution of your products and help manage and mold your developer experience.

Your evangelists should be largely responsible for the success of both your marketing efforts and how well your products serve the developer audiences. Many teams struggle to define which metrics to use to measure the effectiveness of their evangelism efforts, but that's often because they see the evangelist as an individual contributor. Ideally, they should be elevated to a role that oversees the vast majority of the developer experience, even if they aren't necessarily responsible for directly implementing the APIs. The evangelism team may be directly responsible for producing the finalized documentation, maintaining the developer portal, and driving more developers down the marketing funnel. Still, they may only inform the design of the APIs and how well they should perform, rightly leaving the implementation and maintenance of the APIs themselves to the software engineering team.

Since the success of your API program is so closely tied to the efforts of your evangelism team, they should be measured on how well they drive developers through the marketing funnel and how well they work with other teams to improve the overall experience. But you should also ensure they have the tools, budget, and capabilities to produce those results.

The developer marketing funnel

The goal of any marketing strategy is to lead a customer from initial awareness through to completed purchase, including the additional concern of retaining customers long term. Whether you're targeting an external audience who pays to access your APIs or an internal audience you're trying to convince to adopt them, the traditional marketing funnel provides reliable criteria to measure your success.

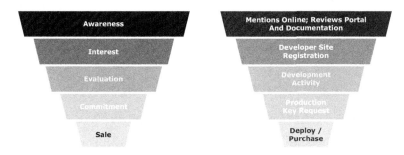

Figure 11. Traditional marketing funnel

The marketing funnel doesn't change much from audience to audience; each step leads closer to a sale with some significant drop off along the way. Moving developers through each stage, however, does require an approach that differs from your traditional audiences. In the previous chapter, we talked about the process a typical developer goes through as they determine what tools and technologies to adopt. That process maps well to the marketing funnel, and there are key activities you can perform and track at each stage to encourage adoption and to capture an eager audience.

Tracking your success at every stage of the funnel is critical in helping you refine your marketing activities and developing a better understanding of how to best serve your customers. The trick is identifying the actions a prospective customer takes to indicate they have moved to the next stage. Each organization approaches lead scoring and tracking a little differently based on the goals of their business, so it's important to understand what you're trying to measure and why before blindly adopting KPIs.

Building awareness

Developers are as susceptible to standard advertising practices as any other audience. If you hit them with enough impressions, eventually your name will stick. To be effective, however, you must associate your brand with a solution the developer is likely to need at some point.

This seems obvious in writing, but is far trickier in practice. Design your APIs to cover different use cases and address many challenges, including those you can't accurately predict. Marketing for every possible solution will create chaos for your marketing campaigns and likely over-segment your marketing, possibly confusing the market. Focus your messaging instead on the values unique to your APIs and the data and functionality they represent.

Consider as an example an API that sells sports statistics. The use cases are many: providing detailed post-game information for sports media, providing real-time statistics for live broadcasts, and providing real-time statistics and odds for sports betting. If you create your messaging to target each of these groups using channels such as Stack Overflow, you'll likely only attract those developers who are specifically working on a project that covers that use case. Delivering messaging that you're the best option for sports betting, for example, may make those building a fan service application believe your solution is not suited to them or that you don't take that audience as seriously.

Instead, broaden the message and focus on the real-time, accurate delivery of sports information and statistics in an easy to implement format. The focus on the data and reliability of your services will be enough for those seeking this kind of information to pay attention.

This bit of advice is based on marketing API programs in dozens of organizations—but it may be wrong for your situation. The only way to know for sure is to build a strong internal practice of tracking all of your marketing activities and comparing the success of different campaigns and tactics until you focus on the ones that drive the most valuable customers to your program. Developing the messaging and marketing plan for your API program, or for any product you intend to bring to market, is not a one-time fire and forget situation. You must constantly experiment and refine your messaging based on consistently measured results.

How you measure these results, especially in the awareness phase, is largely dependent on how you're broadcasting your message. Effectively building awareness for your API program requires putting your message out where developers are most likely to see it. Not all forms of advertising work equally well.

Traditional ad placements

Driving along Highway 101 in Silicon Valley can be a surreal experience for visitors. The billboards along most highways tend to advertise products targeting the general public: restaurants, grocery stores, upcoming movies and events, and interesting local attractions. Once you reach the stretch of highway between San Francisco and San Jose, however, the billboards all seem to become more "techy," advertising databases, technical consultancies, websites, gadgets, and esoteric technical products for a niche audience.

You can see the same trend on the sides of buses and streetcars roaring down the streets of tech hubs like the Bay Area, Austin, Seattle, and others. The effect is amplified during tech-centric events like SXSW and Dreamforce. And while the death of the technical print magazine industry is only slightly exaggerated, you can still find many of these publications filled with ads targeting programmers.

Though traditional display advertising has dropped in popularity for targeting developers, it can still be effective when the message is well-honed and the placements make sense. Where it fails, though, is in the ease of tracking its success. Any attempt to measure reach, the average number of cars driving past a billboard site, the number of issues of a magazine in circulation, the average viewership of a television show, is little more than a rough estimate.

One trick is to provide a call to action specific just to that ad or campaign, a purpose-built landing page with a custom URL, or a keyword to enter on the site. When this action is taken, you can be reasonably sure it was the result of someone seeing and acting on the ad tied to that action.

If you are thinking of using traditional display advertising to drive developers to your program, use caution. For a more mature program with some existing brand awareness, it can be very effective. For the vast majority of

API programs, however, it's not as effective as other tactics.

One glaring exception to this, however, is internal API programs. If your goal is to evangelize APIs as an easier solution for your internal developers, then creating fun and engaging print "advertising" that appears where your engineers work and congregate can not only generate interest and encourage adoption, it can also signal leadership's commitment to a new path forward.

> *The marketing challenge for an internal program is to convince long-time developers used to the "way we've always done things" to adopt a new style of development. Analog advertising supports these efforts well.*

Pay per click and online advertising

The Internet fundamentally changed the advertising model in two powerful ways: it allowed for much tighter targeting of customers based on their behaviors and stated preferences, and it allowed for more detailed tracking of customers when they engaged with the ad itself. In the early days, most online ads were placed and paid for based on "impressions", that is, the number of times the ad was shown on a webpage or to a unique user. An advertiser would, for example, buy something like 10,000 impressions from an online site with the hope that at least

10% of those impressions would lead to a clickthrough to the advertiser's site.

The cost per click model made popular by Google AdWords turns this on its head. The AdWords model, now copied by most major online advertising channels, allows the advertiser to target specific search keywords that users use to search Google and display relevant ads. Google only gets paid when someone clicks through on the ad, making it easier for advertisers to budget toward successful conversions rather than guesstimates of how many might click per thousand impressions. Ad aggregators and individual sites have evolved this process to also consider the types of actions target customers take on their site to better segment the available audiences.

The ubiquity of online advertising is also its weakest feature. Most of us who live our lives online have trained ourselves to all but ignore the flashing banners ads and text advertisements that decorate the websites we visit. Online publications often redesign their sites to take this into account and find clever ways to keep advertising front and center to continue to drive clicks and generate revenue to stay in business.

Clever messaging and flashy interactive ads can catch a developer's attention, but not always in a positive way. It can be intensely annoying to scroll halfway through a coding tutorial only to be interrupted by a screaming video averting the reader's attention. This is not to say that all your advertising for developers should be staid and boring. Instead, the core message of your advertising should outweigh the interruption by demonstrating you understand their problems and clearly relating the value of your products.

Even more important than providing the right messaging, however, is a solid success tracking strategy. If online advertising's greatest weakness is its ubiquity, its greatest strength is its trackability. Every visit to every website provides the webserver with a treasure trove of valuable information about the end-user without necessarily personally identifying them. Through patterns in this data—as well as through personalized identifiers embedded in website requests and responses—it can be easy to track every move an individual makes on that site.

The thrill a results-oriented marketer feels about the information available to them must be tempered by users' privacy concerns. Laws like the European Union's General Data Protection Regulation (GDPR) make this a requirement. Complying with the GDPR, and good privacy practices well beyond the scope of this book, require that you do your research and only use vendors who are at the very least GDPR-compliant.

Even after you have addressed privacy concerns, however, any remaining data you can use to target developer customers is tremendously helpful. Craft your messaging to share the right values with the right audiences and drive these audiences to relevant pages on your site or to purpose-built landing pages. Once they have landed on a site you control, you can use popular website monitoring and metrics gathering tools to understand the most common actions taken by developers and to optimize their experience to build interest.

Developer-focused events

A developer spends most of the workday in front of their computer. The chance to break away from their machine and meet and collaborate with peers is often welcome as it allows for the sharing of experiences and the opportunity to learn new skills from people who understand them well.

Many developers are allowed to attend at least one event focused on their area of expertise or interest each year. An entire industry of developer-focused events has, therefore, sprung up to meet this demand, targeting just about every type of technology, environment, programming language, and developer persona you can imagine.

The best events are those that not only have relevant talks given by experts in the field, but also ample opportunities for attendees to get direct experience with the technologies on hand. Developers will attentively listen to a speaker and frequently photograph slides they feel are relevant for further research, but they respond best when allowed to get their hands dirty with technology.

Conferences

The technical marketing event calendar contains a vast number of large conferences held throughout the world focused on every aspect of computing technology. Technical conferences typically attract anywhere from a few hundred to several thousand—and in the case of mega-conferences like SXSW, Dreamforce, and AWS reinvent—many tens of thousands of attendees from across the entire spectrum of IT professionals. The organizers of these conferences are often major players in the technology space, technical user groups, or groups such as industry analysts dedicated to producing technical conferences.

Your participation in these events will often be some mix of hosting a booth on the exposition floor, giving a keynote or breakout presentation, conducting a hands-on workshop, and plastering your logo all over the event's marketing materials. The cost for sponsorship is usually only the tip of the moneyberg; you'll need to cover the cost of your own marketing materials for the booth itself, the salaries and travel expenses for each attending employee, and the printing, shipping, and purchase of any branded "swag" items you want to give away.

Given the total cost of sponsoring an event, I'm always surprised by how little strategic planning many marketing departments put into these activities. The stated purpose for most conference sponsorships is to build leads to feed the marketing funnel, but so few of those leads are successfully qualified at the event that ROI can be difficult to recoup.

This is especially true for developer events. While developers have a tremendous amount of influence over the tools and technologies their organizations adopt, they're rarely the final decision-maker or purchaser.

A good conference strategy targeting developers is one that focuses heavily on education and getting a developer to follow up after the event has ended. If your sponsorship includes a speaking slot, find someone in your organization who can go on stage and speak to the value of your APIs and its program, demonstrate how it has helped others across a variety of use cases, and how easy it is to implement. Though fraught with the dangers inherent with spotty Wi-Fi access and temperamental machines or video equipment, a live demo of your APIs should demonstrate this to the audience without much additional input from the speaker aside from providing a narrative.

Developers do seem to love swag, especially items they can use on a daily basis. Apparel like T-shirts, hoodies, and even socks and "beanies", are frequently popular items.

USB adapters, device charging battery packs, and multi-function tools often find their way into most developers' everyday carry kit. These gifts can help drive traffic to your booth and may impress your brand on your audience, but their real effectiveness is questionable.

If you utilize this strategy, you can look at using swag as bait to bring developers to your booth and allow you to demonstrate on an individual level how your APIs can address their needs. Staff your booth with experts capable of answering practically any developer question with a detailed, informed answer. The few minutes a developer spends with your expert may not seem like much, but it can leave an indelible impression that the developer will remember when they do find a need for your product. Keep in mind the opposite is also true. The common practice of staffing a booth with attractive people who know little or nothing about the product nor understand the needs of developers, will at best make you immediately forgettable and, at worst, leave a decidedly negative impression of your brand.

Meetups

Where conferences are often a mass swarm of bodies attending a variety of mini-talks and walking the expo floor, a meetup is a more intimate gathering of typically less than 100 people, often on a monthly or quarterly schedule. I described the average meetup in more detail in the previous chapter primarily as a means of fostering a community of developers. Anything that improves the developer experience can be viewed as a means of marketing to developers, and meetups are among the best examples.

Meetups tend to be more informal than other events, though they provide ample opportunity to build awareness for your brand and your API program. Cost can be as simple as paying for the beer and food provided at the meetup. Organizers are often more than happy to have outside companies foot the bill for refreshments in exchange for displaying their logo and providing marketing materials during the event.

As with conferences, you should send staff who can talk individually with developers and share their knowledge not only of your APIs but, in general, to also build a reputation for understanding your developer audiences. These same individuals should be encouraged to speak at these events on topics that are at least related to the areas your product addresses, if not your product directly. When I speak at these events, I will either cover a common use case or new technology and the best practices of how to address or implement it using my company's products. Do not simply focus on selling your product, but demonstrate your understanding of the audience and how your products can address their many needs.

The people you send should interact with as many attendees as possible during the times set aside for networking. Again, the focus is not to sell but to "talk shop" and listen to their challenges. If your staff can provide any guidance, even if it isn't directly relevant to any of your products, the halo effect can help keep your organization top of mind when they uncover a need you can directly address.

Hackathons

Recall from Chapter 6 that one of the three virtues of a great developer is hubris: pride, at times seemingly excessive, in their ability to use their skills to accomplish anything. No other event brings this out in a developer like a good hackathon.

A hackathon is a unique event designed to allow individuals or teams to compete in writing code that implements a specific technology, addresses a specific challenge, or acts as the kernel for a new business. As the "-athon" suffix suggests, a hackathon is a long-form event often held without any breaks, not even for sleeping, for an entire weekend. A good hackathon is equal parts educational workshop, social networking event, and stamina challenge, often featuring good food and beverages. In many cases, hackathons can even be virtual, further extending their reach across the globe.

There can be a tremendous amount of value in sponsoring, hosting, or even participating in hackathons, but ensure that you have specific goals in mind. Hackathons can be a great way to build awareness of your company and your APIs, the whole experience can make you look "technically cool," and they can also be a recruiting channel for your engineering team.

The best way to understand a hackathon is to attend one and either observe or better, participate. I understand the trepidation a non-developer may have entering one of these events. Still, they tend to be welcoming to all levels of expertise, and there's often a role to be played even for the non-technical marketer. The best developers are often amazing at building incredibly cool and useful technologies, but not as focused on getting the word out effectively. If you attend as a non-developer, consider offering your services to manage the project for the weekend, to validate that the project adequately addresses the needs of the stated audience, or to craft the final presentation to wow the judges.

Most hackathons follow a pretty standard agenda, though organizers often adapt the format to meet certain needs. Most events start with a kickoff event on Friday evening. All of the participants gather to meet one another, hear the rules, challenges, and expectations of the organizers, generate ideas, and form teams. The organizers often give sponsors a short speaking slot of generally three to five minutes to describe who they are, why they're there, and what they're offering to participants to help them with their project. Often, sponsors will judge the final entries alongside the main judges and give their own prizes for the entries that make the best use of the products.

After forming teams, the work begins. Most will begin planning the details of their solutions immediately. Some teams form before the event starts and may already come with some idea of what they intend to build. Others will scramble to come up with a team, idea, and minimally viable solution the first night and get to work as quickly as possible.

If the venue allows for it, many participants will camp out in areas they have set aside for their teams and work at all hours. It's not uncommon to see bodies splayed in hallways or under desks at 3:00 a.m., grabbing a cat-nap in between coding sprints.

Saturday is when the bulk of the work is accomplished, with most developers heads down and focused on their areas of responsibility. If you're providing API access to participants, it's wise to make sure your presence is known and to have an expert on hand throughout the majority of the event to answer questions and handle support issues. With so little time to complete the project, time and efficiency are critical, and you should do everything in your power to keep participants who are using your product from experiencing any delays or issues.

The last day is typically a flurry of activity. Many projects that seemed to be golden ideas on Friday will barely represent the original idea come Sunday evening. It's common for teams to shift gears when an idea doesn't pan out and pivot to some new idea to present at the end. The final deadline for submitting an entry is typically sometime between 2:00 and 4:00 pm on Sunday afternoon. At some point on Sunday, the hosts will gather the judges and brief them on their job. If you are a sponsor for an event, there's a good chance you'll be asked to have someone from your organization sit on the judging panel. You should take advantage of this to get even more visibility during the event and build a rapport with the competitors.

The final presentations and judging tend to feel like a party. Typically, food and certain alcoholic beverages will be served, and the anticipatory atmosphere, mixed with the relief of at least being done, creates ample opportunity to network and check in with the teams. The host will explain the presentation process. Typically, each team gets five minutes to present their idea and demo their solution, followed by about three minutes of Q&A from the judges.

If you sponsor any of your own prizes, pay special attention to those teams eligible to win and make your decision accordingly. After all of the presentations, the judges are whisked away to some dark corner where they can compare notes and decide as a group who to declare as winner. Once the winners are decided, the hosts will first ask the sponsors to give their awards, then announce the official awards. It's not uncommon to see the same competing teams win several sponsor awards as well as one of the top prizes.

Hackathons are a lot of fun, but that should not be their sole purpose. Whether you host, sponsor, or merely attend a hackathon, establish your goals, and design all your interactions around them. For example, a hackathon is a fantastic way to get immediate, raw feedback for how well your APIs serve developer needs. If your documentation is unclear, your APIs slow, your endpoints poorly designed, or your onboarding process a headache, hackathon developers will let you know immediately. Often, the use cases from developers at a hackathon are completely unique from what you might find in the wild, which can test how decoupled your APIs are from common use cases.

Hackathons are also a great way to build awareness of your API program and jumpstart your developer community. If you put your best foot forward and are responsive to the needs of participating developers at the event, they'll likely remember you when they embark on a new project that can use your APIs, or recommend you to their peers. It would be a mistake, however, to count the projects built during the hackathon among your successful implementations. The flurry of activity those API keys see during the hackathon will die down to little more than a murmur come Monday, if they ever see any activity again. You can continue to nurture these developers and communicate with them as you do the rest of your developer audience, but don't count on them to be active within your community after the event has ended.

Sparking interest

In the traditional marketing funnel, after you have gained awareness, you want to capture some activity from prospective customers that signifies their interest. This can be difficult for many products in a traditional sales cycle, but is rather easy when it comes to your API program. When a developer signs up for an API key for your program, they're interested.

This reinforces the importance of optimizing your onboarding experience and providing either a free trial tier or a sandbox. Every ad link, every landing page, and every call to action for developers should drive them to your developer portal and, finally, to an API key registration. You should make sure every incoming link from your efforts is tagged with an attribution that indicates its source so that you can evaluate how well your awareness campaigns are performing. For example, if you're using

Google AdWords and sending customers to a landing page, make sure you can track successful registrations back to that initial ad.

Your developer portal is one of your most valuable sources for attracting new developers. If you follow the best practice of hosting your documentation as simple HTML pages, you can leverage the same search engine optimization techniques and metrics used for your corporate website to measure how well you're driving developers through your funnel. While there are tools that allow you to tie anonymous site visitors to specific user accounts, many developers use privacy programs that confound these systems. Therefore, your documentation should not only clearly explain how to implement your APIs for popular use cases, but it should also showcase the capabilities of your program and take every opportunity to encourage visitors to sign up for a key. An API key should be required to adequately use your API documentation.

Registering for a key signifies interest, but it doesn't necessarily lead to a customer. Many developers sign up for API keys or download new software with the intent of trying it out when they have time. The busy life of a developer often means many of these trials go unused. How you define an "active user" in your system will depend mainly on your program and goals. At this stage, however, even invoking a couple of API calls counts as showing actual interest. Those accounts with some activity have priority over those that register and never make a call, and your tactics for nurturing them should be different.

Smoothing the evaluation process

Unless you require some kind of approval process, it's likely the majority of your API registrants will begin their evaluation of your program with little to no interaction with anyone on your staff. A fully automated process does help you get out of the developers' way, but it offers precious few opportunities for you to create any kind of meaningful relationship with them.

During the evaluation phase, your support infrastructure and documentation must be as accurate and responsive as possible. At this point, developers are evaluating how committed you are to supporting your customers as much as they are evaluating your APIs.

This phase starts at the moment they've completed registration. The confirmation page they see upon a successful registration should point them to the next obvious places to visit to start exploring how your APIs can work with their project. A simple set of links to tutorials covering common use cases along with clear call outs for your support systems—email, forums, social media, phone numbers—will suffice in most cases. You should also send a confirmation email containing the same information.

These same communications should clearly outline the steps they should follow once they have decided to implement your APIs in their production environment. If they already have all the access they could need, state that. Otherwise, describe when and how they should request a production key or any other additional steps they will need to take.

Other tactics include short drip email campaigns that try to anticipate the developer's needs at each stage of evaluation, emails to follow up on customers who registered for a key but whose activity dropped off shortly after, or even direct phone calls to developers to see if your team can provide any personalized help. Consider your developer audiences carefully and implement the tactics most likely to help each audience.

Getting a commitment

After the evaluation period, the developer will likely introduce your solution to the rest of their team to get buy-in, then begin implementing your APIs into their project in earnest. If developers used a free evaluation tier or sandbox, they will need to request a production key from you, indicating their commitment.

If your API is designed to be mostly self-service, the commitment action will likely take one of several different forms. If you're selling access to your APIs, commitment will come when they enter their credit card information. If your API follows an indirect monetization model, the commitment action will come either when you see a dramatic influx of activity on their account or when they make their first call that successfully meets one of the goals for your API.

Regardless of how you measure this, your committed developer customers should be treated differently than your prospects. Once they have decided to implement your solution, they effectively become a customer, and your messaging should be focused less on winning their business and more on keeping their business.

Focus most of your activities at this stage on helping your customers deploy their code and keeping it running smoothly to make their projects successful and drive forward the goals of your program. While a great deal of development may have occurred during the evaluation stage, the real work happens during the production stage. Your support infrastructure needs to be at least as responsive, if not more so at this point, to reduce the time it takes for them to go live.

Closing the sale

In most cases, having your APIs deployed live in a production environment indicates that you have closed the sale with the customer. More complex programs, however, may require additional steps, especially if contracts are involved.

If your APIs are designed to aid in building strategic partnerships, for example, you may have some standard boilerplate contract you use for every partner. A majority of those will likely come back redlined as partners seek the most beneficial win-win between parties. Keep the goals of your program in mind as you negotiate the contract and don't concede to requests you can't support.

Your service level agreements (SLAs) are likely to get the most attention during these negotiations. Chances are high your APIs are core to the success of your partners and customers, so it makes sense they'll be sensitive to potential outages or performance issues over which they have little control. Good communication at every point in your program can go a long way to alleviating these concerns. Give your customers a place where they can check the current health and performance of your endpoints, provide direct access to members of your team who can act quickly if something goes wrong, and be sure to design your APIs to provide helpful and timely errors when something bad does happen.

Retaining customers

Marketing is often so focused on filling the funnel and driving conversions that an organization's most valuable resource, their existing customers, can feel left behind. This is even more true in a successful API program. Once a customer has successfully implemented your APIs, the chances are good you may never hear from them again, until they encounter a problem or leave you for a competitor.

Ideally, your API program should hum along with little need for customers to reach out to you directly. Should any issues arise, you need to remain as responsive in your support as you have been at every other stage. More importantly, you need to ensure your customers are aware of any problems or potential issues as soon as possible. Planned outages, new API versions, and anything else that can impact their code should be communicated quickly and clearly on all channels you provide for your customers to monitor.

Even when things are running smoothly, your customers should hear from you regularly. You should make a point to reach out personally to each of your most active or most valuable customers at least once a quarter to find out how well things are working and to better understand their business needs. You may also consider a monthly newsletter that contains any new information about your

APIs or includes content relevant to your products as well as industry best practices.

To measure the success of your efforts, track the average lifetime of a customer. In the case of your API program, that time starts when you've considered a sale closed and continues until either the present time or when they stop actively using your APIs.

Final thoughts

Marketing can be an effective tool for helping to create and drive the execution of a successful API program. The key is to know your audience. Marketing to developers is not the same as marketing to traditional audiences, and you need to make sure that your marketing organization is aware of these differences and recognizes how to use them to their advantage. It is also not a one-time engagement. You need to market your program throughout its lifetime and include the marketing plan as part of the API lifecycle, a topic covered next. When done properly, not only will revenue be positively impacted, but your developer audience will also be successful and hopefully have some fun during the process.

CHAPTER 9

Understanding the API Lifecycle

At this point, we are now ready to cover what most people probably expected at the beginning—the API development process, key considerations when designing and building APIs, and how to manage and support your API program, and platform, for the long haul. As we have seen, without first focusing on the concepts introduced to this point, the best built APIs are not likely to be successful, both in terms of adoption or longevity. If you don't know what APIs mean to your organization, which support mechanisms to put in place, and how to reach the right audience at the right levels, you won't have a clear understanding of what to design and build to obtain the most value. This wastes valuable time and resources, and may result in disillusionment across the management chain who may perceive the promise of APIs did not measure up.

But, with the value and structure of your API program defined, you can now determine how to incorporate the API development lifecycle into your current or desired enterprise software development model. While a discussion of the virtues of Agile vs. Waterfall, "water-scrum-fall," and other approaches are beyond the scope of this book, we do need to describe key aspects of the API lifecycle and where it differs from traditional software development methods. There should be no surprises here, except for perhaps the focus at the end of the lifecycle on stages that need more attention than what is typically found in traditional software development. I will cover the topics shown in Figure 12.

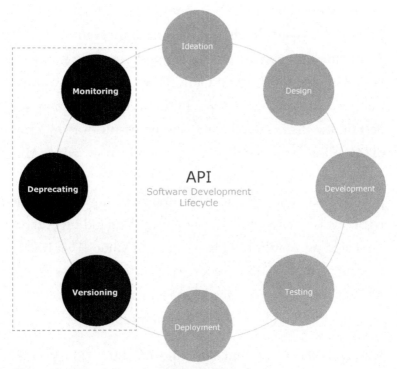

Figure 12. API software development lifecycle

Any API lifecycle will typically include aspects of each item, but the diagram does not imply these are the only steps or that the steps occur in this order. It is advantageous, for example, to test your API contracts as early as possible, even before implementing the APIs. In the diagram, we also highlight three additional areas that require special treatment when it comes to APIs and the associated program: Monitoring, Deprecating, and Versioning.

We cover each component in more detail in the following chapters. But let's now take a look at how they fit together, and how they may differ from the way you look at software development today.

Building applications by assembly

APIs by themselves are not applications. This may be surprising to some, but when is the last time you encountered a single API that made up an entire application? Yes, APIs may and arguably should be products and treated as such, but they are the building blocks of applications. APIs form a platform that developers can use to quickly and easily build applications inside and outside the organization, including at various levels or layers of your technology architecture (we'll come back to these layers in the next couple of chapters). For example, Google Maps is a platform and treated as a product, but it consists of a series of APIs and is not a single application. Developers can use these APIs to assemble new applications that include strong mapping capabilities in a drastically shorter amount of time. After all, who wants to build a mapping application from scratch, when other organizations already do this quite well and make it easy to leverage or extend.

It is this core concept that typically results in variations between the software lifecycle used to support traditional application development and API-based development. APIs are components of applications, and this dependency places extra emphasis on topics such as versioning and deprecation, which make up the tail end of the API lifecycle.

Ideation through deployment

Ideation

The first step, of course, is to generate the ideas for the APIs themselves. These ideas may come from the overall company strategy, various business requirements, partner requests, digital transformation initiatives, and many other sources. The ideas may be gathered using traditional software development requirements gathering approaches, and other techniques, such as the now popular "design thinking" workshop, have proven to be quite effective. I have also found internal API hackathons to be a fun and useful way to quickly test different ideas. Regardless of which approach you take, the key is to focus on the customer of your APIs, whether this is an internal consumer, external partner, or external developer.

Design

API design is a critical step in the process, and one reason why *Chapter 10* is devoted to design. But in general, the first step when designing any API is to identify the use cases. How will stakeholders want to work with your APIs? What business functions are the APIs supporting? Who is doing what, to which pieces of information? By understanding the use cases, you can then start to extract the "nouns", objects, events, or commands that are likely candidates for the APIs themselves, and subsequently move into topics such as URI design, payload formats, use of HTTP methods and status codes, standards selection, versioning, and more. This can be a challenging phase, and also lead to some heated debates! It can be helpful to utilize a form of rapid prototyping or API modeling with request/response or event-driven samples at this point to show participants how their use cases would look as APIs. This quick, visual feedback can help guide the conversation as people immediately see the outcome of the design discussions, and get a feel for how their requirements would translate into an API program and platform. API modeling also fits very well into an agile approach to development, and even starts to create the framework for associated documentation and test cases.

Finally, it is important to include not only the technical team in this design process, but also any stakeholder that has an interest in ensuring that the API program is successful. By opening up the process, you can often obtain a deeper and broader perspective than what an IT group may provide, and also facilitate earlier "buy-in" of the program and approach. Arguably, this last point also proves to be very valuable when developing "traditional" software or applications.

Development

At some point, development of the APIs, along with the supporting underlying services, will begin. *Chapter 11* addresses development in detail, including many aspects that are not technical. Development not only includes the coding of the business logic, but also the creation of mock applications, selection of associated technologies and standards, considerations surrounding the deployment target(s) and associated Continuous Integration / Continuous Delivery (CI/CD) pipeline tooling, source code control, team structure, and even the impact of the organization's culture on development. Remember

Conway's Law?[10] You also have to think about the breakdown of the work, which in a new API program can be quite daunting and overwhelming. Priorities need to be assigned to the APIs and services, and plans put in place for how best to group the APIs into categories or teams. For example, you can start by developing APIs by business function, by creating the read-only APIs followed by read-write APIs, or other groupings.

Regardless of the approaches, it is, as always, important to communicate early and often to stakeholders. I've seen many projects where the developers "disappear" for some time without any form of communication or information sharing with the sponsors or business owners of the program. This lack of communication can place a cloud of uncertainty around the program, and lead to questions about the value and the money being spent on the API project.

Communicate early, and communicate often! Regular checkpoint sessions, status updates, full transparency (even when facing issues or time pressures), and the use of demonstration sandboxes can all assist in ensuring that the program and associated development is viewed positively.

---

[10] Conway's Law: Organizations design systems that mirror their own communication structure. https://bit.ly/2SP35W6.

Testing

Testing is involved in multiple stages of the API lifecycle. You cannot wait until the end of development to test—a much more agile approach is needed to capture issues early and validate the API design. It is much cheaper and easier to discover early on that an API design does not meet expectations rather than at later steps in the process—not unlike today's software development approaches and strategies. You not only have testing of the defined API contract, but also the supporting business logic, payloads, error handling, status codes, security, monitoring, performance, and all the other aspects that make APIs easily consumable and thus more successful. All this testing cannot all be done towards the end of the cycle—at least not without significant cost! Testing must be intermingled with the rest of the API lifecycle stages.

One recommended starting point is to use mock apps to allow testing of API contracts before the underlying service(s) are built. Mock apps allow internal or even external consumers to see if the contracts meet their requirements, properly model the desired interactions, and are easy to use and understand. However, mock apps are not just about the contract; they should also contain some dummy data or responses so that the corresponding payloads and any related standards or business guidelines can be validated. I have also found it useful to have these mock apps available for a period of time, often the same period of time as the actual APIs themselves. This allows you and your customers to test breaking and non-breaking changes, subsequent versioning, and other items that don't require the entire underlying API implementation.

It is also beneficial to start applying API authentication and authorization techniques against the mocked APIs. Test not only the APIs themselves early in the process, but also the supporting security configuration. It is much cheaper to identify and correct security issues now, as opposed to after the APIs have been deployed to production against production data!

Error conditions, business functionality, performance, and graceful degradation in the face of system or other application issues are also obviously important. Don't forget to test any related dependencies, such as other APIs upon which your new API is based. This type of testing can go many levels deep in your overall technology architecture, so be sure to drill down as needed.

One final note pertains to documentation. Because each API's associated documentation will be important to the success of your API program and platform, you must also include it in the testing process. Auto-generate the documentation as much as possible, but also ensure that it is readable, easy to follow, relevant, and describes how an API consumer can get assistance.

Deployment

In today's world of cloud-native development approaches, IaaS, PaaS, and FaaS solutions, containers, and a myriad of other technologies, the importance of automation in the API lifecycle cannot be overlooked.

As is often mentioned and discussed in the IT community, the goal is to automate as much as possible, and when you think you have automated everything, automate again.

The rapid growth of Continuous Integration and Continuous Delivery (CI/CD) techniques and technologies is an indicator of how important automation has become to organizations.

But in numerous cases, I have seen organizations stress that they are Agile in their software development practices, but in actuality, they are only Agile in design (perhaps), development (most likely), and some types of testing. However, once integration or system testing arrives, or the software is set to be deployed, the process becomes sequential and various projects are thrown over the fence into a global queue for a single operations group to package and deploy. This "water-scrum-fall" approach may seem Agile, and the right terminology is typically used to describe it, but it is often not optimal because the back-end of the lifecycle is effectively a bottleneck that can curtail any previously achieved gains in time and cost.

In many organizations, it can be very difficult to suddenly switch to a culture of "two-pizza teams" overnight. And, as mentioned, you need to consider your culture in addition to organizational structure, regulatory requirements, and geolocation. But culture is an important factor to consider and optimize, especially given the nature and rapidly changing business requirements that today's API programs and platforms must support.

The tail-end of the lifecycle

When it comes to the API lifecycle, three components need to receive more focus compared to traditional software development practices. This additional focus stems from the fact that APIs are mostly used to assemble or enable applications and are not applications themselves, and thus have a potentially deep graph of dependencies both internal and external to the organization. A strong approach and strategy for versioning, deprecating, and monitoring can make or break the success of your API program.

Versioning

Versioning, along with discussing on how to best use REST (and now GraphQL, along with other approaches likely to emerge in the future), are probably two of the most heated topics in the API community. Strategies such as versioning through the use of the URI, custom headers, query parameters, and content negotiation are often debated, and in many cases veer towards almost religious debates. I discuss versioning in more detail in *Chapter 10*, but for now, just know that it is important to determine a versioning or API evolution strategy. The strategy should cover how to handle breaking vs. non-breaking changes, define when a new version is required, identify what triggers each type of change, and specify how a change will be communicated.

Deprecating

Related to versioning is API deprecation. At what point do you remove or deprecate an API? How long do you support the deprecated API? What do you do about developers or partners that seem to refuse to move away from the old version? And how do you determine what to deprecate anyway?

These questions and more are important to consider as part of any API program, especially for APIs that are envisioned to survive for an extended period—and you wouldn't be doing all of this work if you didn't think APIs had long term value! This can be an odd item to discuss at the beginning of an API program because you typically don't think about shutting down a service before it is even written. But the potentially pervasive nature of APIs makes it important to have a deprecation strategy and, more importantly, to formalize this strategy so that it can be conveyed to API consumers. Communication has been mentioned a number of times in this book, and it will be mentioned again. Having a well-defined and published approach to versioning and deprecation will go a long way to ensuring developers and partners are not surprised.

That said, however, in my experience, someone is *always* surprised. At some point, a customer will discover that their favorite API has been deprecated, and slightly panic. At this point, you will need to be ready to briefly "turn back on" an API, offer some sort of extended support (often at a cost to the customer), offer migration assistance, or in the extreme case, you may choose to do nothing at all. The decision will be dictated by considerations such as the maturity of your program, associated revenue, reputation risk, and other business factors. But this is likely to come up at some point and needs addressing by key stakeholders.

Monitoring

The final aspect of the API lifecycle is monitoring. Monitoring includes obvious functions such as measuring latency, throughput, response times, uptime, and other system metrics. But monitoring in this context also includes several other metrics which, as previously discussed, may be used to determine and prove the success of your API program. They include API usage, data volumes, active consumers, revenue impact, and the associated LTV and ARPU measures. Chapter 3 discusses these metrics in detail, but in summary, it is important to define, continuously evaluate, and use them to drive improvements as necessary.

For example, a sudden drop in usage may indicate a problem with an API (relatively simple to address), or a broader shift in the market (more problematic). The right level of monitoring can tell you when to look at deprecating an API, or it can tell you that more APIs for a particular business function would be valuable. Combinations of API calls can also be quite informative; the analysis of API event and web logs might show patterns or correlations of usage that can identify new business opportunities, or be a leading indicator of a potential issue or threat.

Finally, for APIs that are consumed internally, monitoring can help stakeholders demonstrate how APIs are reducing costs, speeding time to development, or driving revenue directly or indirectly. Monitoring can and should provide detail about your program, point out areas of improvement, and provide an idea of the impact the program is having on the overall customer experience.

Final thoughts

Understanding and successfully incorporating the API lifecycle into your organization and its software development strategy is the first step in realizing the potential of your API program. While there are many similarities to the traditional software development lifecycle, there are also differences in areas such as versioning, deprecating, and monitoring. Recognizing and adapting to these differences will go a long way to helping ensure that you are providing API consumers with the right levels of functionality and service.

CHAPTER 10

Discovering and Designing Your APIs

As with any application, the level of effort put into your API design should easily pay for itself later in the lifecycle. With the right approach, your APIs will be more flexible, performant, scalable, meet customer requirements, and quickly adapt to changing business needs and market demands. Conversely, a poor design will result in a brittle solution that is difficult to use, error-prone, and quickly dismissed by the developer community. Let's, therefore, start by looking at those components that underpin solid API development.

Throughout this and subsequent chapters, I'll do my best to stay away from common and sometimes heated debates when it comes to specific technologies in this area. Do you use SOAP vs. REST vs. GraphQL vs. whatever? Support versioning through URI or custom headers? Use OpenAPI with or without JSON Schema? These debates, evolving trends, and incompatibilities will always exist—it's the nature of technology. Instead, I will provide guidelines to keep your APIs clear, consistent, and secure. If teams are starting with the assumption that your APIs will follow one popular format or another, they're starting on the wrong foot.

So, what exactly does API design involve? You have the obvious considerations, such as the objects, data, and functionality that an API should expose, along with the standards and protocols that are selected and followed during development. But there are also various related considerations, such as where the API itself will sit in an architecture, as well as security, scalability, monitoring, supported interaction patterns, and error handling. Some considerations will directly impact the API's design, while others are related to the services that support the APIs. This chapter will cover both because separating the concerns of the supporting services (called "microservices" in today's language) from the API design can be challenging. Often, the team involved in writing the API contracts is also involved in the design and development of the underlying services.

During the design and development processes, distinguish between the API layers (potentially associated with a corresponding API gateway or management component), and the implementation of the supporting services.

Service implementation should not be dictated by the API contract, API gateway, or management layer. By keeping the layers separate, you can achieve greater flexibility, less lock-in, greater choice, and allow each layer of the stack to evolve separately.

To start, how do you determine what should be built in the API platform? I will use common REST concepts and other approaches to illustrate various points in the discussion, but again, the intent is not to teach you REST or any of the other emerging frameworks. Instead, I will focus on the aspects of design that you need to consider to build clean, concise, and easy to use APIs regardless of the framework utilized. We next examine API protocols and standards, followed by considerations for versioning and security. By the end of this chapter, you should have a good understanding of how to approach API design, and how to carry this design forward into the next stages of the API lifecycle.

Identifying what to build

The beginning of the API design journey starts with user stories. These stories will uncover the needs of the consumers to be addressed by your APIs. Remember that you are designing your API to support this audience, so it is important to consider their characteristics. Create these stories in collaboration with developers and all stakeholders of the program. All these perspectives will help ensure a consistent understanding of the requirements, and clear up any confusion around business terms, data requirements, and other factors.

User stories and business domain modeling

User stories, as used in agile development, are a great way to determine the capabilities that the API platform will need to support. The stories should not imply any sort of technical solution, but rather help stakeholders understand what data or functions might be required for an API consumer to do what they need or want to do. They may also convey how these consumers will want to query information, manipulate data, and traverse data relationships.

The stories should also stay away from preconceived notions about what is or isn't possible within an existing technical environment. I've seen cases where user stories were not presented because the business team "just knew" that their current data model could not support the desired functionality. They had struggled with certain projects in the past, and so built this idea up in their minds, even though it was not 100% accurate. Physical database tables, current applications, and other legacy technical debt, should not limit the user stories nor drive the design of the APIs. Prioritization and cost-benefit analyses for these stories can occur later in the process. You first want to start by getting all of the desired capabilities out on the table.

As a couple of quick examples, and without meaning to suggest any specific approach to implementation, you may start with user stories like the following.

> *"As a developer, I want to use an API to retrieve product summary data for a product category so this information can be displayed to a customer."*

> *"As a consumer of a product category API, I want to display product categories and related product data so that it can be verified by a product owner."*

Through user stories, you want to identify a set of defined objects and start to map these to the API capabilities that will be built and deployed. In these examples, I used objects and personas such as "customer," "product owner," "product," and "product categories," and these are likely candidates or entities that will be represented by your APIs.

Drilling down into the user stories and looking at the data required to support them will surface whether a data element is a simple property, a field of an entity, or its own entity. For example, using the above examples, it may look like "categories" could be a simple attribute of "products." However, because a category tends to have its own set of information, such as name, sub-categories, and associated product counts, it likely makes sense to treat a "category" as its own entity, and simply provide a link between it and "product." Of course, you can take this line of thinking too far and start to over normalize, so it is vital to use the stories to help you determine whether to promote a data element to its own entity.

You can start to derive how to manipulate data through user stories. It is likely, for example, that you will want to perform CRUD operations against products or change how to group products into categories. Or determine how certain data elements are related (for example, products may exist within one or more product categories).

Entry points become evident (there is a desire to start with "product" and "product category"), and the types of queries will also begin to emerge (conveying filtering or parameter details). The key is to use these stories and the related discovery process to try to understand the needs of your API consumers before implementing your APIs. This sounds obvious, but it is not always that easy, especially given factors such as increasing business demands and time constraints. The tendency is to start implementation immediately, but you need to understand at least some basics first, before jumping into development. Note that this process should not take months or even weeks; after a few discussions, you should have enough detail to start showcasing how the API will behave using a variety of prototyping tools or mock apps.

Further defining the design of the entities

While defining entities and directly related capabilities, you also want to expand your view to other related design topics, such as filtering or parameter passing, data hierarchies and traversal, and error handling. Note that these topics are also technology-agnostic. Evaluate specific technology features when the desired capabilities are understood, some of which are covered later in this chapter.

Throughout this part of the process, one key consideration is consistency. Establish and stick to a pattern because nothing will kill a program faster than having APIs that don't follow a consistent pattern. To borrow from a simple REST example, is it */products/12345* or */products?id=12345*? For GraphQL, is the mutation named *createUser* or *userCreate*? Stay consistent, and your API consumers will thank you.

> *Test your resulting API design against as many use cases and user stories as possible, and as early as possible.*

Creating and exposing mock apps based on your designs will help, as will inviting various developers from your target audience to provide feedback early in the process. Even so, it is likely that some of your initial designs will change over time—a good reason to have a well-defined versioning or API evolution strategy established.

Data hierarchies

Understanding relationships between the data that will be represented by your APIs is critical during API design. Which data elements or entities are related to each other? Which entities are typically accessed together? How will API consumers wish to traverse or "walk-through" the data and associated relationships? What are the typical starting points for a data hierarchy?

Answering questions such as these will tell you a lot about how API consumers expect to access and work with the data exposed by your APIs. For REST APIs, this understanding can help determine the design of your URIs, use of nested resources, unique identifier strategy, and filter parameters. With GraphQL, these answers are also important because they influence items such as schema design and caching strategies.

> *Regardless of the technology used, understanding the data and how it will be reflected in your APIs is a critical success factor.*

Errors and response codes

Just as naming, data hierarchies, request structures, and payload formats are essential to API design, so is the way that errors are handled and conveyed to the API consumer.

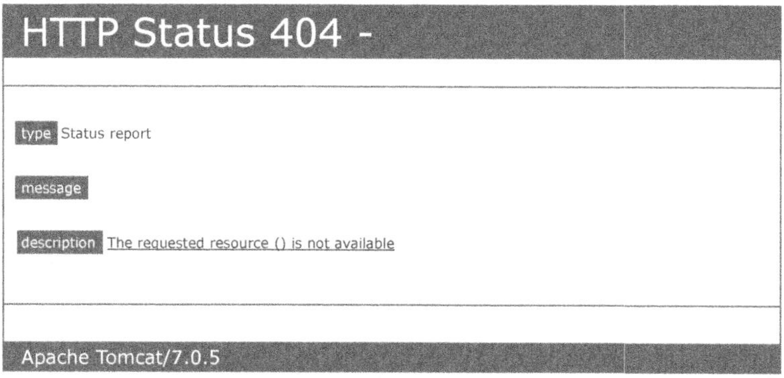

Figure 13. A Not-So-Great API error

Improve the experience for your API consumers by not only documenting known error conditions, codes, messages, and possible resolutions, but also returning appropriate programmatic responses to calling API clients. These responses make it easier for developers to understand what is happening with your API, and where to look for potential issues.

Decide whether to include (and how to include) errors in the schema or response payload. If HTTP is the communications layer, then incorporate the corresponding HTTP response codes into the error handling strategy. But what about situations where the error is not related to a server error or other type of client issue? If the error is related to data that failed a business validation check, how will this be conveyed back to the API consumer?

For example, in the case of a REST API, it is recommended that the API doesn't simply return generic codes, and expect the API consumer to figure things out! In some cases, it can be advantageous to use the HTTP response codes as a form of error category, and to include additional status information in the response body. Using the previous example, an attempt to add a new product that already exists (according to the unique identifier) may result in an HTTP 409 error ("Conflict"), with the response body including a more detailed description of the exact nature of the error. This method provides additional information to the API consumer and makes it easier for them to determine the exact cause of the error without having to dig through pages of documentation or reach out to support. This same set of considerations applies regardless of the technology used, so make sure to include a comprehensive error handling strategy as part of your API design.

Usage patterns and placement

When designing your APIs, it is helpful to understand the placement of the APIs in your technology environment, and the usage patterns they will need to support. While this knowledge mainly impacts the implementation of the underlying services, it may also affect your API design. For example, at one time, designing an API seemed to imply that developers would use "REST over HTTP" (or even "SOAP over HTTP" if we go back a few more years), but this is no longer the case. APIs do not equate to REST, and they do not have to use HTTP.

APIs today can be synchronous or asynchronous, as seen through the AsyncAPI initiative.[11] This initiative creates standards for defining asynchronous (event-driven) APIs, which is very similar to what exists today for synchronous REST APIs with the OpenAPI specification. APIs can be consumed by a variety of endpoint types with varying capabilities, utilized to facilitate data self-service or data as APIs functionality, or be defined to support other design patterns such as the backend for frontend (BFF) pattern.

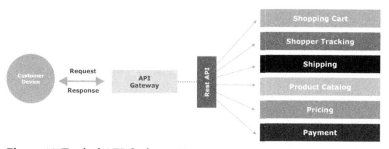

Figure 14. Typical API design pattern

---

[11] https://www.asyncapi.com/.

Each of these patterns and placements can influence the overall design and development of your APIs—from the API contract to the associated aspects of payload design, error handling, communications protocol, and performance or caching requirements. APIs are everywhere!

Scanning the API landscape

There are many approaches available to organizations for defining and creating APIs and API platforms. I will not attempt to list all of them here, but it is important to be aware of the API landscape and to understand how to evaluate or determine what best fits your needs. It's part of the fun of being an API architect!

Common examples from the API landscape today

One of the most common decision points in API design is which architectural "style," language, or specification to use. In this loosely defined group, there are approaches such as RPC (https://bit.ly/2YQeyZ4), REST (https://bit.ly/2WieaAY), GraphQL (https://graphql.org/), OData (https://www.odata.org/), JSON API (https://jsonapi.org/), and AsyncAPI (https://www.asyncapi.com/). I've excluded SOAP (https://www.w3.org/TR/soap/) from this list, because

SOAP APIs have been rapidly replaced by so-called "RESTful" APIs, and REST (at least some form of it) has become the de facto way that developers create APIs today. However, just as APIs do not always mean "request/reply," they do not always equate to REST (or HTTP). Other options are available, and some, like GraphQL, are gaining traction.

Secondly, you have various options for API payload formats, including XML, JSON, and protocol buffers (commonly referred to as "protobuf," see https://bit.ly/2SRO9Gv). XML is considered legacy in many circles, and now often only encountered when working with older backend services, private/internal APIs, and SOAP interfaces. JSON arguably has the most traction at the moment, with formats such as protobuf commonly used in conjunction with gRPC for internal or private API communications.

Thirdly, just as definition languages emerged to support the use of XML documents with SOAP and web services, such as XML schemas/XSDs and web service definition language (WSDL), there are now various definitions to support the creation of JSON payloads that are typically associated with today's APIs. With JSON Schema (https://json-schema.org/), for example, you can define the structure of your JSON documents, and use the schema to validate payload data against this structure. A GraphQL schema, utilized with the GraphQL API query language, is

232 • API SUCCESS

used to describe the types, queries, and mutations that are valid within that system.

And finally, various standards and specifications have been created to define how to best approach API design and development. Initially, it is worth clarifying that REST is actually an architectural style and thus has no set standard. Regardless, it does have several published guidelines and best practices that have been defined over the years, given its popularity and maturity, along with associated models such as the Richardson Maturity Model (https://bit.ly/3dsDQAA).

REST is often utilized with the OpenAPI (formally Swagger) API specification (https://www.openapis.org/). OpenAPI has become the standard way to describe REST APIs as it includes details on API metadata, paths, security, servers, reusable components (such as schemas, parameters, and links), tags, and documentation. This specification is programming language-agnostic and is an important specification for the REST API community. An OpenAPI document describes an entire API via YAML or JSON, and allows API consumers to use an API with little knowledge of the underlying implementation. It also allows the various API vendors and open source community to create interoperable tools to support developing and documenting APIs against this specification. If you are building RESTful APIs, it makes sense to look at this specification.

As described on the OData website, OData (Open Data Protocol) is an *"ISO/IEC approved, OASIS standard that defines a set of best practices for building and consuming RESTful APIs. OData helps you focus on your business logic while building RESTful APIs without having to worry about the various approaches to define request and response headers, status codes, HTTP methods, URL conventions, media types, payload formats, query options, etc. OData also provides guidance for tracking changes, defining functions/actions for reusable procedures, and sending asynchronous/batch requests."*

Originally developed by Microsoft in 2007, OData provided a standardized way (REST-like) to access enterprise data sources via HTTP. OData defines a server-side data model, utilizes a metadata document to describe the exposed resources, and allows client applications to access OData services through the OData protocol.

For example, an OData client could use REST-like OData resources to retrieve or perform CRUD operations against a resource (such as, *GET https://services.odata.org/v4 /TripPinServiceRW/People*),[12] or you could use more complex SQL as part of the request (*GET https://services.odata.org/v4/TripPinServiceRW/People? $top=2*

---

[12] OData "Step 1: Requesting resources" sample at
https://www.odata.org/getting-started/understand-odata-in-6-steps/.

& $select=FirstName, LastName & $filter=Trips/any (d:d/Budget gt 3000)).[13]

OData is still present in some organizations today but has since fallen out of favor. It is seen when interacting with enterprise applications that expose interfaces via OData, or in situations where there is a need to expose a traditional common data access layer, where this layer is subsequently hidden via another API layer so that OData specifics are not exposed to consuming clients.

GraphQL is the "new kid" on the block. Created by Facebook, GraphQL is often touted as a replacement for REST. However, the answer is not that simple. GraphQL at this time is not an API architectural style, but rather a draft specification for a query language and execution engine. This makes GraphQL stricter than REST, which is both its advantage and disadvantage.

Since there are many articles on the Internet that compare GraphQL with REST, I won't provide yet another comparison. However, the one comment I will make is to make sure the comparisons you review are including or considering *properly* designed REST APIs, not just "REST-like" APIs. Yes, understanding the full capabilities of REST and HTTP can be difficult, and this in itself may be a

---

[13] OData "Step 3: Queries" sample at https://www.odata.org/getting-started/understand-odata-in-6-steps/.

justification for using GraphQL in certain scenarios, but REST with HTTP already solves many of the shortcomings that are present in GraphQL today. And remember, the decision point is not necessarily GraphQL *or* REST. There may be a place for both in your API platform.

Factors to consider during selection

It should be evident by now that the choices are many, and there is no simple answer to the question of what you should use as the basis for an API platform. It is also possible no one choice is the right choice; your solution might consist of multiple approaches depending on use cases and desired functionality.

> *Dig into the capabilities of each approach, use user stories to prioritize what you need, and build prototypes. Just be prepared to pivot, and do not get tied (or blindly follow) one approach over another. By taking a rational approach to your evaluation, you can increase the chances of success for your API platform.*

In addition to the topics already covered, you may also want to use the following questions to guide your selection. Your responses will hopefully direct your attention to an appropriate option(s), or at least provide a great starting point.

⇒ *What data types do you need to support with your APIs?*

⇒ *Are your APIs purely internal, or will they be exposed to external parties or partners?*

⇒ *What type of API consumers will be using your APIs? Target devices?*

⇒ *What type of backend services will be behind your APIs? Pure microservices? Databases?*

⇒ *What performance requirements do you have for your APIs?*

⇒ *How complex are the data relationships and data hierarchies? How often do these change?*

⇒ *What type of security is required for your APIs?*

⇒ *Do you have restrictions on the API consumer or back-end programming languages?*

⇒ *What type of interaction patterns do you need for your APIs? Request/reply? Event-driven?*

⇒ *What communication protocol(s) are appropriate for your APIs?*

⇒ *Do your APIs need to cross different "bounded contexts"? Communicate or work with different organizations or groups within the enterprise?*

Security

Security is an important aspect of API design, regardless of whether the APIs are exposed over the Internet to external parties (public APIs), or are used to facilitate internal service interactions (private APIs). Again, there are several options available to the API architect for security, including common approaches such as TLS, various authentication and authorization schemes such as HTTP basic authentication, API keys, OAuth2 (https://oauth.net/2/), OpenID Connect (https://openid.net/connect/), and other strategies supported by common API gateway or management platforms. As with the various protocols, frameworks, standards, or specifications associated with the API landscape, it is important for API architects to be aware of the different forms of API security, and to carefully consider the capabilities of each as part of the development of the API platform.

Versioning

The last big topic for this chapter is versioning. How do you know when to deploy a new version of an API? What approaches are best when it comes to providing API consumers with a mechanism for accessing certain versions of an API? Or are versions even needed? Again, the API architect has several options available, and it is essential to weigh the pros and cons against one another to determine the best fit. For example, we need to consider versioning options for REST APIs and how these considerations change with GraphQL. Regardless of the approach taken, remember to review this topic early. Sorting out a versioning strategy after your APIs are deployed, in production, or in use, can be a challenging proposition. Best to avoid the headache as much as possible.

Why a new version?

A variety of factors can trigger the need for a new version. Typically, a new version is needed when a "breaking" change is introduced into the API system. A "breaking" change is essentially a change that "breaks" the code an API consumer had to write to specifically support your APIs. This may include a datatype change (for example, integer to decimal), a change in the response data format, the introduction of additional/mandatory keys, changes to the URI structure, or any part of an API that is removed. Minor changes, conversely, don't typically require a version change, such as the addition of an endpoint.

Regardless of what triggers the version change, it is important to communicate the change to your API consumers through various channels. Don't just update the API documentation and hope that everyone will automatically adjust, or even be aware of the new version. Proactively reach out and work with your community to ensure that they understand the change and its implications.

Versioning with REST

Versioning through URI path

A common approach to REST versioning is to use URIs to point to a specific version of the API. Adopted by organizations such as Facebook, Twitter, and Airbnb, this approach allows clients to easily cache resources as the cache keys (URIs) are changed as versions change. This approach, however, does result in longer URIs:

http://www.example.com/api/1/products

https://api.twitter.com/1.1/account/settings.json

Versioning through query parameters

The second approach is to utilize query parameters to version the API. This approach is straightforward to implement, and it is easy to default to the latest version if the query parameter is not specified. However, given the use of the query parameter, routing requests to the appropriate API can be more difficult:

http://www.example.com/api/products?version=1

Versioning through custom headers

In this approach, include the version number as an attribute in a custom header. This doesn't clutter the URI with version information, but it does require the developer to add the custom header, and the server to parse this information:

> curl -H "Accepts-version: 1.0" http://www.example.com/api/products

Versioning through content negotiation

Finally, you can version through content negotiation. This allows you to version a single resource and doesn't require URI routing rules, but it is less explicit, harder to cache, and requires HTTP headers with media types.

> curl -H "Accept: application/vnd.example.com+json; version=1.2.3" http://www.example.com/api/products

Versioning with GraphQL

Version through evolution

GraphQL takes a different approach to versioning, although it can be versioned just like any REST API. It focuses on the idea that a "versionless" API is possible through evolution. According to the GraphQL documentation:

> "GraphQL only returns the data that's explicitly requested, so new capabilities can be added via new types and new fields on those types without creating a breaking change. This has led to a

common practice of always avoiding breaking changes and serving a versionless API."[14]

Thus, in theory, you can add new fields, and since API consumers specifically define what fields they want in the response, this should not cause the API to "break" because existing consumers will still get (and only get) the fields that they previously specified. Once they are ready for the new fields, they can update their query and receive the new data. Techniques like nesting can also help to make it simpler to make changes to a GraphQL schema, and you can deprecate fields to indicate that they should no longer be used.

I should also mention that it is possible to evolve a REST API. It simply depends on the nature of the change, and if there are things that can be done behind the scenes to either mask the change or provide API consumers with more time to adjust. Regardless of the techniques used, remember that *any* change can be highly disruptive. Consider the impact on your customers.

Final thoughts

Throughout this chapter, we focused on technology-agnostic considerations while not getting caught up in

---

[14] https://graphql.org/learn/best-practices/.

specific design considerations for REST, such as resource endpoint design, the use of HTTP verbs and response codes, and HATEOAS as a way to describe valid next states. We also stayed away from other approaches such as GraphQL (mutation input design, nesting, caching, and others). Technology will change, and thus this book focuses on the underlying concepts as opposed to technology. Regardless, by discussing various design considerations and related topics, this section emphasized that even the newest of technologies does not short-circuit the need for good design.

CHAPTER 11

Building your APIs

For many developers, this step in the API lifecycle is the most fun. So much so, that there is often the temptation to short-cut aspects like design and rush to this step, arguing that this is how "Agile development is done," "mock apps will drive the design," or "today's API frameworks eliminate the need." If you hear any of these statements, be very wary! Of course, you don't want to over-design and spend time in "analysis paralysis," but you do want to make sure you understand the core requirements of what needs to be built, for whom, and under what restrictions or considerations. Jumping to a popular code library without this background and understanding can lead to poor API performance, poor scalability, and subsequently poor adoption of your APIs. You want to avoid "architecture by resume," and let the design guide your code, not the other way around.

This chapter is not a coding tutorial. There are plenty of Internet resources for learning how to utilize a particular code library. It will, however, introduce you to various options that should be considered when turning designs into code. It reviews key steps in the API development process, looks at the ways APIs can be created, tested, and deployed, and discusses various API-related architectural concepts and patterns. By the end of this chapter, you should have a good understanding of how to approach API development, and how to carry this result forward as you support and manage your APIs in the future.

The API development process

Figure 15 shows a typical API development process. Variations will exist, but this sequence of phases represents the typical cycle that organizations go through when building their APIs.

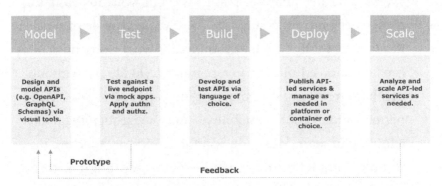

Figure 15. API development process

Model

The API development process will typically start with one or more API models. These models are intended to allow the API architect or developer to describe the details of the identified APIs in a standard manner before writing code. This programming language-agnostic approach describes items such as allowable payload formats, associated schemas, URI paths, expected error responses, and other properties. The degree to which the models describe your API, and the format or specification that you select, will depend on your needs and use cases. For example, if you are defining a simple API model to allow internal services (microservices) to exchange information, you may decide to represent the data as protocol buffers (https://bit.ly/3cl2pPE)—simple, straightforward, and commonly used, such as when interconnecting core services via a protocol like gRPC.

For cases where it makes sense to build your APIs using techniques such as REST or GraphQL, you may utilize more comprehensive approaches, such as the OpenAPI specification or GraphQL schemas. As discussed in the previous chapter, the OpenAPI specification has become the standard way to define REST APIs, while a Schema Definition Language (SDL) is used to define GraphQL schemas. In these cases, the resulting models will not only provide a comprehensive description of how your APIs function, but also may be used as inputs for facilitating or automating mock app development, documentation generation, client/server code generation, and other capabilities. More details on these automated capabilities are provided below in the discussion on the Build step. On the other hand, if an event-driven model is required, then an AsyncAPI definition will make the most sense. Similar to the role of OpenAPI for REST APIs, the AsyncAPI initiative is focused on standardizing the definition of asynchronous or event-driven APIs, and also supports the automatic generation of various developer assets for this style of API.

Regardless of your needs, after API design, the creation of your API model is the next critical step in the API lifecycle or development process. Spend some time getting this model right because it will form the foundation of your coding, testing, and documentation efforts. It is also vital to pick an approach that has the backing of the industry in general, to help improve interoperability, avoid lock-in, and ensure that your APIs will survive the test of time. This book has used a few of the common approaches that exist today to illustrate certain points, but they will change over time. It is up to the API architect and developer to be aware of these approaches and determine the best fit(s) for their program.

Test

It may seem a bit odd to discuss testing before building, yet it is critical to test your defined model as early as possible in the API development process. As previously mentioned, it is important to get the model right, as any mistakes or omissions will become apparent as APIs are consumed, and discovering these issues during or after the coding process is expensive. Thankfully, the approach of building "mock apps" enables API architects and developers to test their models before implementation is complete, saving time and money while the model is iteratively refined.

A mock app is a test application, typically auto-generated from an API model (and then perhaps enhanced via code) that may be used by API consumers to execute API calls against "mocked" systems and data, and to receive representative responses. These API consumers may be simulated, or they may be part of a test group that is internal or even external to the organization. But regardless of how the mock app is consumed, it should represent the real API as much as possible. The underlying business logic will not yet fully exist, but the way the API is called, the generated responses, and even any returned errors should be as close to the production implementation as possible. By standing up a mock app, an API development team can receive early feedback on the defined API models and determine if the model behaves as expected when used by the intended consumers.

A mock app is also an excellent opportunity for API architects and developers to apply and test authentication and authorization strategies with limited risk. If an API is breached at this point, the impact should be minimal; no real data is exposed, and no real systems are impacted.

Creating mock apps, especially from common model definitions associated with OpenAPI, GraphQL, and AsyncAPI is typically straightforward. Use tools such as Visual Studio Code (with the appropriate extensions), Swagger Editor (https://bit.ly/3cjD5tj), or the TIBCO Cloud™ API Modeler (https://bit.ly/3dA9qfX) to generate the model, and then feed this model into various open source or vendor tools for the automatic creation of a mock app. As always, there are a number of tools for this purpose, and some are better than others.

First look at the tools that support your selected API modeling approach, compare this list to what the industry is using, and then download and try one or two tools with a real-world example. For example, OpenAPI related tools may be currently found at https://openapi.tools/, while GraphQL tools are listed at https://graphql.org/code/. If you do look at vendor tools, make sure they support open standards—you don't want to get locked into a vendor-specific language or approach because if later you need to move for some reason, you want to be able to move to another tool with the least amount of rework possible.

Finally, mock apps may not just be temporary. It can be valuable to leave mock apps running in a test environment, even after the developed API is in production, because this makes it easy to onboard new customers, test versioning or API evolution strategies, or quickly demonstrate API functionality. But by the end of this mock app prototyping cycle, you should be fairly confident that your models represent the designed features of your APIs.

Build (and test again)

You are finally at the point where you get to build something, which is the most tangible part of the process — the development of the code that will support the APIs. Developers have a wealth of choice. It is easy to get lost in the latest and greatest GitHub project or be confused by the vast amounts of marketing around API platforms and capabilities. As mentioned previously, let the design drive your decisions and your code.

This step is also based on the API model. Just like there are tools that assist with the generation of mock apps, there are tools that assist with generating both API client and server code. For example, if generating an API that uses gRPC and protobuf for communications and data passing, you can generate supporting classes from the proto file (using the protocol buffer compiler) and subsequently use these classes within your API implementation.

Similarly, for the OpenAPI and GraphQL specifications, there are tools that can autogenerate client and server-side code. My recommendation here is the same as for the mock app creation step: select tools (vendor supplied or otherwise) that fit your use cases and support open standards. For example, the npm graphql-tools package (https://bit.ly/2xSnrGC) and openapi-generator (https://bit.ly/2Ael7KS) are common open source tools for GraphQL and OpenAPI development, as are tools such as swagger-codegen (https://bit.ly/3dBRx0l) and Project Flogo™ (http://www.flogo.io/). This, however, barely scratches the surface of available tools, and this list will change over time, so be sure to do your research.

For debugging, you have to consider various components, such as client-side debugging (using, for example, the browser console/developer tools), network monitoring (at the client, or between the client and the back-end API implementation), logging and monitoring on the server-side, and the use of proxies (such as mitmproxy and various other products) to assist with introspecting and debugging web traffic.

Of course, the build step not only includes the API implementation code itself, but associated documentation, a CI/CD strategy, unit testing, and deployment. You can use your model with tools like swagger-codegen, bump.sh (https://bump.sh), and redoc-cli (https://bit.ly/3dv149b), to automatically generate documentation from an OpenAPI specification.

The use of automated tools is important in this context because you want to ensure that any produced documentation remains in sync with the API model and code, and by using automated tools, this step can be included as part of an overall CI/CD pipeline. Note that the documentation can also be enhanced by using self-documenting coding practices when building your APIs. This would include the use of techniques such as GraphQL's introspection features and hypermedia controls with REST APIs. Finally, a streamlined CI/CD process that performs the tasks in Figure 16 in an automated fashion can also simplify development, reduce errors and manual tasks, and improve code quality.

Figure 16. Streamlined CI/CD process

Tools such as Maven, Jenkins, Jest, JUnit, Postman and many others can be used to build an automated build-test-deploy cycle. Time spent here is well spent. As the number of your APIs grows, and as multiple teams start to collaborate on the APIs in various ways, having a well-defined CI/CD process will be very beneficial.

Deploy

Where and how you deploy your APIs is the next important aspect of the API build process. As previously discussed, deployment should be part of your CI/CD strategy. But that is just the tip of the iceberg. To what platform are you deploying? Are you using private or public cloud infrastructure? Containers and/or container management platforms such as Kubernetes? Will your code be run in a JVM, NodeJS, or as a Go executable? Do you need a GraphQL server? Or perhaps Envoy (https://www.envoyproxy.io/) or some other type of service mesh? How about a vendor API management platform? And how will you ensure security, monitoring, high availability, scalability, and all of the other "-ability" items that are important to any API platform?

Lots to think about! I wish there was one "magic" answer, but as you know, the choice is not that simple. I think we can agree, however, that deploying to "bare metal" (a physical computer server) is no longer the best option, and even deploying directly to virtualized hardware is typically not the first choice. Instead, it is likely that you are going to deploy to a cloud platform, whether a private cloud based on containers and a container management system like Kubernetes, a public cloud environment like AWS, Google, or Azure, a vendor SaaS environment like the TIBCO Cloud™ Mashery® API management platform, or some combination thereof.

The majority of cases I see today in the enterprise are hybrid. Some APIs are public, while others are private and used for internal purposes. Even when using various deployment targets, enterprises don't want to manage multiple environments with different support requirements, training needs, and operational considerations. This is one of the reasons why containers and Kubernetes (K8S) are becoming common approaches to deploying software applications, including APIs. Code, regardless of the programming language, can now be deployed into a shared and common base foundation, whether it is on-premises or on a public cloud. Base support, training, and operations stays consistent, and it is easy to incorporate this approach into a CI/CD pipeline.

Of course, the world of APIs also has a number of specific, additional capabilities that will be required to some degree, including what is typically provided by an API gateway or API management platform. This includes features such as developer portals, traffic management, security management, API bundles and plans, monitoring, reporting, user management, document hosting, and so on. These features are covered in more detail in later chapters, but for now, when it comes to deployment, and if you are looking at a vendor platform, you want to ensure that it is based on current cloud and container technologies and has a strong roadmap for the future.

Adopting a platform that does not match your cloud strategy and direction, or was not designed to fit into today's world of microservices, cloud-native applications, and APIs, will likely result in operational headaches and greater "technical debt." These same comments also apply to open source. Regardless of what one might be told, open source is not free when you consider total cost of ownership (TCO), and open source can still lead to technical debt and solutions that are difficult to support. Open source projects can die, developers can leave, systems can go down at 3:00 am, and surrounding technologies can change or become legacy.

Ensure that you pick well-known projects and broadly utilized industry vendors, frameworks, and approaches to limit risk.

Scale (and monitor, manage, and measure)

The last step in the API development process (we are also now blending into the aspects of API operations and support) is how the APIs will scale and grow to support increased demand. Of course, I'm confident that if you have followed the guidance in this book, increased demand will be a natural result of your program!

From a development standpoint, not only do you need to make sure that your APIs can scale, but also any related or supporting technologies. These can include back-end databases, enterprise applications, mainframes, caches, OAuth servers, proxies, logging/metrics collection systems, developer portals, and others. Yes, you may be able to spin up another container behind a load balancer to support increased API consumer demand, but are the underlying services and technologies able to support this increased load? I've seen many cases where a related but forgotten component could not handle the increased load (including items such as mainframes and even log collection services). Thus the auto-scaling aspect of the API platform did not matter. The backend pieces were not able to match the demand.

You need to make sure that all components and layers are scalable, especially if one is initially unsure of what to expect (during, for example, your equivalent of the retail industry's Black Friday).

Finally, as you develop API services, remember to incorporate hooks and other mechanisms to facilitate monitoring and measurement of the APIs. API usage, fields used, response times, data volumes, request trends/patterns, and uptime are all important metrics to consider when deploying your APIs.

These hooks become even more important with approaches such as GraphQL, as in this case, you have one entry point into a GraphQL server that may, in turn, trigger several calls behind the scenes, and these calls may result in network traffic between multiple locations or sites. If you are not aware of what needs to happen on the server side to fulfill the original request, this can quickly lead to performance issues that are difficult to trace. Thinking about this early, and incorporating Application Performance Management (APM) techniques and proper tracing, correlation IDs, and other needed approaches, can make life much simpler once an API is deployed. As previously discussed, such metrics can also facilitate versioning, API evolution, and deprecation—all important aspects of your API program.

Architectural patterns and approaches

We have covered the API development process along with key decision points and considerations when turning your API designs into reality. But before moving to the next chapter, it is important to understand various API-related architectural patterns and approaches. APIs are not just about allowing external API consumers to "add to cart" or "checkout". APIs can be utilized to support various popular enterprise application contexts, and understanding these contexts and the role that APIs can play will help you build solutions that deliver broader and deeper ROI across your API program.

Layering with APIs

In many enterprises, you are likely to encounter multiple "layers" of APIs. These layers may be defined or created for a variety of reasons, including the need to support different types of API consumers, promote clear separation of concerns, support distributed API development and responsibilities, accommodate mergers and acquisitions, and align with organizational structure. The layers may be owned by one or more groups, and even consist of different API technologies.

Figure 17 shows, as an example, how an enterprise could utilize REST APIs to expose core business, application, and data domains, and then layer a GraphQL API on top for use by API consumers.

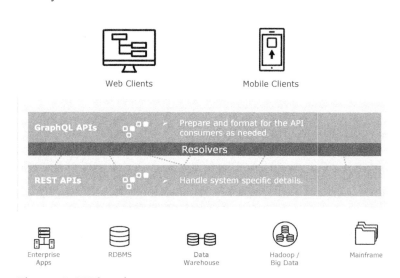

Figure 17. API layering

Assuming there are clear API models, this would allow each API layer to evolve separately (even through different teams), and enable developers to pick and choose the right technology for the right set of use cases. Each layer has a specific role, may evolve independently, exist in an on-premises, private, or public cloud context, and may be owned or managed by single or multiple teams. Layering is also a core principle of the Backends for Frontends (BFF) pattern that was first described by Sam Newman (https://bit.ly/3cvcw4s). With this approach, there would be a supporting API (BFF) per user experience or per type of user experience—iOS, Android, web, desktop, and others. The BFFs would be maintained by the team that also supports the user experience, and utilize other API layers as the source of their information and data. There is no one size fits all approach when it comes to APIs. You need to find the best combination that fits your use cases and the overall enterprise.

Asynchronous/event-driven

In some cases, APIs may be message or event-driven, and not based on request-reply interactions. For example, an API consumer may wish to be pushed data the moment new information is available, instead of needing to submit an originating request or perform some form of polling. Or an API client may wish to publish data for delivery to one or more consumers, where the number and location of consumers is not known to the client at the time of the publication. This type of behavior is not new. It has been around a long time and commonly referred to as messaging or publish and subscribe. But the ability to treat these types of endpoints in a standardized fashion similar to REST APIs is now becoming a reality.

The AsyncAPI initiative, as introduced previously, is focused on allowing API architects and developers to create a standard definition or model of an event-driven API. Similar to the OpenAPI specification for REST APIs, the AsyncAPI specifications allow for the definition of event-driven APIs in a programming language and protocol-agnostic manner. Figure 18 shows that this approach to API development can be combined with traditional request-reply interactions.

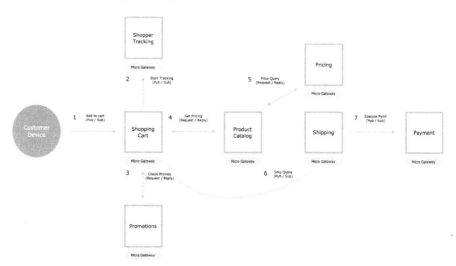

Figure 18. Combining API interaction styles

This combination provides API-driven organizations with the best of both worlds in a hybrid or multi-cloud fashion, with broad support for various protocols, interaction patterns, streaming, loose coupling, and both synchronous and asynchronous communications.

Data as APIs

As the volume of data collected by organizations grows, and as these organizations look to derive greater value from their data via interactive visual analytics, self-service analytics, artificial intelligence, machine learning, and augmented reality, it is becoming increasingly important to allow some form of standardized access to the data. The data may sit in different types of storage technologies (cloud and on-premises), and require access through a variety of mechanisms—not everything is based on languages such as SQL. APIs, when combined with techniques such as data virtualization, can make it easier for consuming applications and other users to discover and access data for their needs.

Figure 19 outlines the use of data virtualization technology to catalog and connect to various data sources, define and secure common "views" of data across these sources, and provide high-speed access to the data represented by these views through a set of generated APIs. This scheme standardizes access to the underlying information, allows views to represent actual business domain objects (as opposed to exposing raw table or file structures), and eliminates the need for expensive ETL (extract-transform-load) jobs. Data consumers no longer need to know where the data is, data sources may be independently added or removed from the defined views, and security (row and column) may be applied in a layer that is separate from the underlying data sources or consuming client applications. It is also possible to monetize data through these APIs, thus adding to the business case for a related API program.

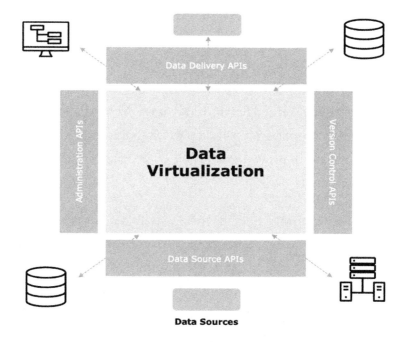

Figure 19. Data virtualization

Microservices/Function as a Service (FaaS)

Today, the services upon which your APIs sit are commonly called "microservices." This term has become somewhat overused in the industry and so has many potential definitions. But in general, microservices are a way of building software components that are independently deployable, stateless, bounded by business context, and elastic. They are often described as "products, not projects," and are a way of breaking a traditional monolithic application down into smaller, reusable, and properly bounded IT components. You can think of microservices as a way to build enterprise capabilities that are composed of collections of smaller, independently deployed software components written in a variety of programming languages. In today's world, it is also likely that these components will be part of an automated CI/CD pipeline, and deployed in a public or private containerized environment.

This architectural style fits nicely with an API platform and associated API program. For microservices to be effective, they should have a well-defined and managed set of APIs. These APIs may expose microservice functions to external consumers, or they may be used internally to deliver a variety of enterprise capabilities. Microservices can be synchronous or asynchronous, and should have associated models, security, and developer documentation. Given these parallels and close synergies, a strong API program is, in many ways, also a key factor in the success of a microservices architecture.

You can take this concept further by decomposing microservices or business capabilities into even smaller components or "functions." Functions, deployable in frameworks such as AWS Lambda or Azure Functions, typically perform very specific units of work, so their deployment and scaling can be done at a very fine level of granularity. Also, unlike a microservice that often incurs a cost whether or not it is performing work at any given time, functions typically only incur a cost when they are invoked. If they are idle, there is no charge. Of course, it is not possible (or desirable) to decompose every enterprise application into separate functions. Still, in some instances, it can be advantageous (both from a cost and performance perspective) to take this approach. How would a client invoke these functions? Through APIs, of course!

Service meshes and microgateways

Related to the microservices concept described above is the emerging notion of a "service mesh." When moving to an environment comprised of potentially dozens or even hundreds of distributed microservices, it can be challenging to configure, network, and debug the interactions between these services. A service mesh allows deployed services to remain agnostic of the network. Network services and other features such as network-level routing and load balancing, filtering, security, rate limiting, logging, and tracing are provided by the mesh, leaving the microservice to concentrate on the application and associated business logic.

As shown in Figure 20, the API-led microservices are deployed in containers (for example, in a Kubernetes environment that is configured with a service mesh add-on), and the service mesh (Istio in Figure 20) is used to manage the communications and related functions. This scheme eliminates the need to build this type of logic (which is often duplicated) into the services themselves, and also simplifies the configuration of properties such as timeouts, retries, and the rollout of new microservice versions.

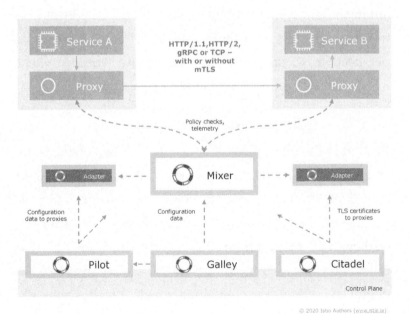

Figure 20. Service mesh

Do you need a service mesh? Service meshes and associated implementations are in the early stages of adoption. It is possible that these capabilities will eventually become part of popular container management environments such as Kubernetes, or that the features will gradually be rolled into today's API gateways and management platforms. However, as API and microservices environments grow in complexity and size, and as the technology matures, a service mesh (or something like it) may become the standard way of deploying these types of solutions. My suggestion is to be aware of the technology, follow the associated trends, and look for the future convergence of the technology with your use cases.

Sagas

The final consideration we will cover in this book when utilizing APIs to expose key business functions or services is the concept of a "saga." For example, imagine a scenario where an API is invoked by a point of sale (POS) device to activate a mobile phone for a customer. Behind the scenes, this single request may trigger a number of APIs, including APIs to update the customer's details, establish a billing account, provision the hardware on the network, and any number of other functions. The order in which these APIs are called is likely dependent on several factors, including the customer profile, product type, and associated promotions. Therefore, the order of API execution is not set at design time. The actual order of calls is something that needs to be established dynamically and on-demand. Certain API calls may execute in parallel, some may execute sequentially, a mix of synchronous and asynchronous calls is possible, and all need to be completed before the order is deemed to be successful.

How would you dynamically assemble the path of API calls? Correlate responses with requests, and identify situations where a response does not come back at all (for example, due to a system failure), or doesn't come back within a given service level agreement (SLA)? Various approaches are possible, but in these situations, I have often found it useful to use a declarative approach to API choreography. This approach typically uses states and rules to dynamically assemble (at run time) the correct series of APIs to invoke, as opposed to procedurally defining all possible combinations at design time. Responses are correlated with the original requests, and each "state" can track required SLAs, or even detect the fact that a request, response, or event is missing. Together, the states and rules form a "saga," or an end-to-end picture of how a particular order (in our example) needs to be fulfilled. States are typically persisted, which makes it easy to determine where an order is stuck, and real-time dashboards can be presented to highlight areas of potential bottlenecks or issues. You can either assemble this functionality using combinations of tools, or certain types of event processing platforms like TIBCO Cloud™ Events software, are capable of providing this form of API coordination, which can be very useful when dealing with numerous APIs and dynamic environments.

Final thoughts

Building your APIs is one piece of the API puzzle, and obviously, an important piece because it's where the conceptual work we've described to this point becomes a reality. As noted, the journey can be confusing, with the risk that the program may quickly explode when it comes to time and cost. Fortunately, there are several well-known and well-documented industry standards and specifications that can assist, along with numerous resources across the open source and vendor community. Go back to your user stories, refer to your design, and let this drive your code. Automate as much as possible, and test early and often! By doing so, you will build, test, and consistently deploy APIs, and continue to drive the success of your API program.

CHAPTER 12

Supporting Your API Consumers

You've done it. You've worked hard to justify and sell your API program, carefully progressed through the steps of the API lifecycle, and deployed a set of APIs that are now ready to be used by external (or internal) API consumers. But, did you plan and establish a part of the program for supporting your API consumers? Do you have adequate documentation, samples, software development kits (SDKs), and support processes? And are these processes appropriate for your target personas?

Even the best designed APIs can trip up developers and API consumers. This chapter focuses on strategies and approaches for supporting your API consumers, and how you can minimize the effort required to learn and adopt your APIs. These approaches include the effective use of developer portals, documentation, tutorials, and specialized technical support. This chapter also presents strategies for streamlining communication between API consumers and your development teams, and how to reduce your support workload and associated costs.

Remember, a key part of the customer experience is not just the API, but the surrounding materials and processes.

Documentation and tutorials

As introduced in *Chapter 11*, as APIs are developed, it is important to ensure, typically through automated processes, that the documentation matches these APIs. An automated CI/CD process is key since tooling can be incorporated into a build pipeline that autogenerates many technical components of the documentation, including associated API descriptions, parameters, endpoints, and related authentication requirements. Example requests, responses, or events should be included, along with potential errors and error conditions. Of course, this technical documentation is just one aspect of the overall content to provide to your API consumers. The broader picture, which includes the developer portal, is discussed later in this chapter.

In many cases, it is also useful to include tutorials as part of your documentation set. Each API tutorial typically focuses on a single topic. When brought together, they provide a quick and easy series of "how-to" steps for the developer that may be practiced in a local or cloud environment. The format of these tutorials may be simple, such as text and code snippets on a single webpage, or they may use video and more interactive web experiences. Keep in mind that creating videos or more complex tutorials may be costly and time-consuming and not provide a corresponding increase in benefit. Hard to edit formats are also challenging to keep in sync with the APIs, and thus are prone to early aging, quickly reducing their value as time progresses.

Keep it simple, remember your target personas, and most importantly, keep the materials up to date as your APIs and program progress. There is nothing worse, relatively speaking, than a tutorial that doesn't work in the end because the API calls or logic are out of date.

> *Have the documentation and tutorials created by people that match the profile of your API consumers. If your target is developers, then have developers create the material, as they will speak the language that your target audience understands.*

Code samples and SDKs

Along with documentation and tutorials that describe the APIs, it is also useful to provide code samples that demonstrate how to solve common problems. Need to demonstrate how to invoke a complex GraphQL call or mutation? Want to provide examples on how to handle nested JSON responses? Or showcase how to utilize API keys or other authorization techniques, and handle errors and any related recovery steps? Code samples can be used to demonstrate all of these aspects of your APIs and more.

As mentioned in *Chapter 6*, developers will look for ways to simplify their lives and reduce overall development effort. Good code samples can do this, and reduce support requirements and costs at the same time. If your API consumers can get answers to common questions from clear and easy to consume code samples, it reduces the load on your support staff. It also helps ensure that users will speak positively about your program in the communities and forums in which they are active.

However, like the other topics discussed in this chapter, it is important to keep these samples up-to-date, ready-to-go, and as close to real-world examples as possible. Do not expect developers to take your samples and then perform substantial work to make them production-ready. It is more likely that a developer will use your samples as-is, and then, if things do not work as expected, it will likely be seen as a reflection of the quality of your APIs, and not of the samples themselves. Ensure that the code samples accurately reflect how they should be used in production, are provided in possibly multiple programming languages, and are continuously improved as experience is gained on how your APIs are consumed.

In certain cases, it may also be beneficial to provide a SDK over a range of your APIs. This SDK may wrap complex functions into simpler functions that are more native to a particular programming language, and make it easier for developers to consume your APIs in their applications. Again, the goal is to make it simple for your API consumers to get started, leverage the exposed API calls, and use these capabilities in the manner they want to use them, as opposed to being forced into a certain style or programming language.

Support and feedback

At some point in your API program, it will be necessary to provide support to and collect feedback from your API consumers and developers. Communication and bi-directional interaction are key. If developers feel that their requests are simply going into a black hole, or if none of their feedback is incorporated into your API program, they will quickly shift to another solution or organization they see as being more responsive and attentive. This is obviously true for external API consumers, but it is also true for internal consumers.

If internal application teams do not receive the right levels of support or responsiveness, they will typically find workarounds or simply develop their own capabilities, leading to duplication of efforts and inconsistent approaches to API-led solutions. But what is the right level of support? And how do you collect feedback?

Support

The processes and structures for supporting your API program can take many forms, but the key to success is first to understand your target audience. Creating a support program that targets the citizen integrator or enterprise developer can be very different from the level of support required by hard-core open source developers. This understanding is necessary to ensure that the right level of support, via the right mechanisms, is being provided to the right people. Furthermore, in some cases, you will have more than one target persona, and therefore it will be important to segment your audience so you can again provide the right level of support to the right people.

Your API documentation, tutorials, and samples are, of course, one aspect of support. These are the timeliest and, quite frankly, cheapest form of support, and thus essential components of your program. At some point, however, these mechanisms will be insufficient for solving a particular issue or question. Therefore, you also need to have a well-defined support process to ensure that nothing falls through the cracks.

Mechanisms need to be defined for collecting, recording, and distributing support requests; appropriate people must be notified and assigned to the requests in a timely fashion; responses must be logged and communicated back to the requestors; and metrics must be collected to measure the support process and identify areas of improvement. These mechanisms should be documented, published, and made available to all people involved because they will not only ensure that the right steps are being followed, but also assist when training new or additional staff for the API program. You may also choose to make some portion of these documented processes available to your API consumers so that they understand the process, have visibility into what's next and feel comfortable with the type of support they are receiving.

As to the structure of the support organization, it is common to use a dedicated team, and if you do, this team must be able to communicate and work closely with the API development teams. You may also consider having a member of the development team rotate through the support team for a period of time, to transfer knowledge, assist with complex support requests, and give the development team first-hand knowledge of the challenges being encountered. Finally, you may also choose to have dedicated technical resources for a particular group or customer, especially if they are a key consumer or a large portion of your API traffic. The exact structure will depend on your organization, but having blended teams can be a very effective way of executing an overall API program support strategy.

As you will see later in this chapter, having a developer portal can simplify these interactions and provide a single touchpoint or location for all related communications. You want to automate as much as you can so that you can spend more person time on the requests that matter, and on the unique or unforeseen use cases. You also want to ensure that relevant and related support information is conveyed to the API program stakeholders and developers so that improvements can be made, automation can be increased, and better documentation and samples can be created.

Feedback

Collecting feedback from your API consumers is also key. Without feedback from your users, you will often be guessing about what is needed from your APIs. These may be educated guesses supported through the analysis of collected metrics, usage patterns, and overall API consumption statistics, but direct feedback from the people using your product is one of the best ways to provide focus, identity features, improve prioritization, and spot trends in your direct audience and related industries.

Of course, not all feedback is positive, and it can be human nature to focus on the positive rather than the negative. Equally address both positive and negative feedback, and even consider giving certain types of negative feedback a faster response because it can spread quickly throughout related communities and forums.

Address the feedback, let people know you have heard them, and show that action is being taken, even if the action is a simple explanation as to why things are the way they are.

The mechanisms by which feedback is collected can take many forms, including via a developer portal, online user groups, customer support, or even dedicated customer committee meetings or roundtables. It can also be useful to make certain feedback items public, typically after a review by internal API program stakeholders. Regardless of how it is collected, it is important to turn this feedback into decisions and (if necessary) actions, even if the decision is to do nothing. I've seen many cases where feedback is collected, lists are generated, but nothing is done, which defeats the purpose of collecting the feedback in the first place. To an API consumer or developer, it can be exciting to see that their feedback was taken seriously and drove actual change and improvement. Leverage this excitement to invigorate your API program and prevent it from going stagnant.

Bringing it together

Providing documentation, tutorials, code samples, support, and feedback mechanisms are all important aspects of supporting your API consumers. But how do you tie it all together? What is the most effective way to expose these materials and capabilities to your audience without triggering high costs, consuming large amounts of resources, and providing a disjointed user experience? Through an API developer portal, that's how!

A developer portal can be used to successfully encapsulate all of these capabilities in a single location, while at the same time reducing your support workload and requirements. This portal is typically web-based with functionality openly exposed to the general community, and additional functions or customizations controlled through authentication, user-based roles, and access rights. It is a central place for all information regarding your API program and can be utilized to streamline the API consumer experience for both internal and external audiences. The portal, especially for external consumers, will also likely be branded in a way that is consistent with other external-facing channels (such as an organization's public website). However, the branding will likely be "turned down" a level to make sure that the experience is not heavily marketing-driven.

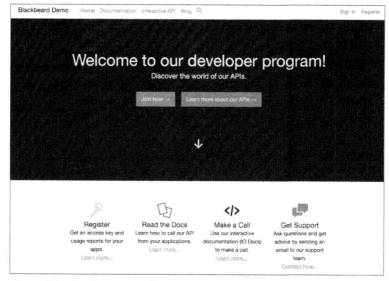

Figure 21. Developer portal

Over the years, I have seen many developer portals, some better than others. Successful portals share a few common traits, some of which are listed below. Remember, the goal is to streamline the API consumer experience, increase self-service and automation, and provide the right information to the right audiences. If your portal is not providing these benefits, then it is likely that one or more of these traits needs to be reviewed and addressed.

- This is obvious, but the portal should be uncluttered, easy to navigate, and have a simple, clean design. If information is hard to find, or if a feature is not easily accessible, users will quickly become frustrated and look elsewhere, or they will burden your support staff with unnecessary requests and questions.

- Content should be built using standard HTML constructs and single-page/scrollable content (no special plugins should be required). It should follow a responsive design because your audience will likely use different browsers and devices when interacting with your site.

- It should be evident from the initial landing page how first-time visitors can get started with your APIs. Links to features such as related documentation, API key requests, contact information, login pages, and demonstration capabilities ("try before you buy") should be easily visible and accessible. Self-service capabilities, such as the ability for an API consumer to request or recover issued API keys, should be provided.

- A link to an API status page, which includes the current status of any issues under investigation, should be provided. This allows API consumers to quickly determine if some sort of technical issue is impacting any APIs they are using.

- The API technical documentation should be easy to access and navigate. As discussed, this documentation should cover various aspects of your APIs, including requests, responses, payload formats, parameters, errors/error codes, and related examples. Code samples and SDKs should be clear and linked to the relevant parts of your APIs, and if multiple programming language samples are included, it should be easy to switch between these samples.

- Any related assumptions or other usage guidelines should be described. For example, what is your versioning or deprecation strategy? How will API consumers be notified of changes or upgrades? What limits exist when using or consuming the APIs (typically relevant when issuing or allowing demo capabilities)?

- The process for obtaining support should be clear and tailored to the role and type of user accessing your APIs. For example, the support process may be defined in one way for a trial user, and in another way for a registered enterprise customer. This process will map back to the overall support strategy and process discussed earlier in this chapter.

- Similarly, the process for providing feedback should be clear and customized to the general or authenticated user. Any associated notifications should be easily accessible and viewable in the portal.

- All portal content should be easily searchable, including any related blogs or discussion forums.

- Additional content, such as a change history or FAQ, can also be provided.

Putting together these capabilities from scratch can be daunting, and thus many organizations may choose to narrow the functionality and provide only the bare minimum of features. However, today's API management platforms greatly simplify the creation of these portals, include templates that are easily customized, and often bundle many or all of the features listed.

Some platforms even offer advanced features such as integration with external marketplaces (for example, the AWS Marketplace), which can provide another outlet for allowing your API consumers to discover and consume your APIs. Whatever approach you select, make sure that you focus on your personas and select the features that will be most relevant and useful to the execution and support of your program. Automation is key; you don't want to manually manage an entire API program, especially if it grows rapidly either internally or externally.

Final thoughts

A developer portal is not the place to market to your users! Running a marketing campaign or promotion through the portal is likely to negatively impact the overall developer experience, so be sure to think twice before using the portal in this way. Also, remember that the topics and capabilities discussed in this chapter are relevant whether your target API consumers are internal or external (or both) to your organization. Many of the same concepts apply and are needed by your own developers as well as those that are external to your organization. The portal is an extension of your brand and should reflect the right level of professionalism, ease of use, and information delivery. Without it, it will be a challenge to scale your program for any moderate to large scale API initiatives.

CHAPTER 13

Real-world API Management

In the last chapter, we covered the use of various materials, artifacts, and processes that are extremely valuable for supporting your API consumers. Throughout this book, we have also discussed the API lifecycle, covering everything from ideation to deployment. To complete the story, we will now put various concepts together that are related to the general notion of API management. Bits and pieces of this topic have been covered in various chapters of this book, but let's bring them together and understand what it takes properly manage APIs.

Managing an API program goes well beyond simply controlling who has access and how to provide real-time support. An entire industry has emerged that promises to help address a majority of API management concerns, but no tool can cover it all. In this chapter, I explain what API management looks like in the real world, discuss the considerations you'll need to evaluate as you deploy your APIs, and arm you with the knowledge to evaluate what tools you may need to buy or build to make managing APIs, well, more manageable.

By the end of this chapter, you'll understand what it takes to properly manage your APIs, monitor their performance and success metrics, empower your staff to help your API consumers and identify opportunities for improvement, and evaluate the tools on the market to find the right set that fits the needs of your organization.

What Is API management?

API management is a series of capabilities that surround API implementations and support their deployment internally or externally. Every API deployment needs supporting management functions, from managing users to monitoring and reporting. Whether acquired by purchasing a commercial API management platform, by building certain capabilities in-house, or by deploying a combination of the two, some aspects of API management are required to ensure that your API program does not become a tangled web of manual effort, diverse scripts, security risks, and configuration files.

Again, the functions included in such a platform can vary, but typical capabilities include:

Capability	Description
Ability to manage users, roles, and other inward-facing security controls.	Security in this context includes the management of any defined enterprise users or roles that administer APIs through the platform. You must be able to control the platform functions that users can see or manipulate, and also support integration with external enterprise authentication or authorization systems such as LDAP.
Ability to define, map, and configure endpoints, plus bundle APIs into plans or products.	API platforms can provide various configuration settings for API endpoints, including the mapping of internal to external API URIs, routing, security, error handling, header support, timeouts, and many other settings. Many platforms also provide support for bundling or grouping individual APIs into plans. This allows various settings to be applied to the plan as opposed to the individual APIs, and for offering the plan as a product to external consumers for simplified packaging or monetization.
Ability to manage API traffic and communications.	API platforms often include traffic management features such as caching, the ability to secure and mediate API related traffic (internal and external), SSL support, CORS (cross-origin) configuration, and header configuration.
Ability to manage API keys and other aspects of outward-facing security functions.	Includes the ability to manage API consumer accounts and external-facing authorization/authentication strategies such as HTTP basic authentication, API keys, or OAuth2 and OpenID Connect schemes. API security was discussed in *Chapter 10*.

Capability	Description
Ability to manage and distribute API documentation.	This topic was introduced in *Chapter 12*. API management platforms often provide a mechanism for hosting and distributing any related API documentation, samples, SDKs, and tutorials to your API consumers.
Ability to define and host a developer portal, including support for forums, FAQs, documentation, testing, and sample code.	This topic was also covered in *Chapter 12*. A developer portal can be a very effective mechanism for hosting and distributing the various artifacts that are generated in support of your API program, as well as for providing a centralized location of reference and communication for API consumers.
Ability to monitor and report on API metrics and performance.	Throughout this book, I've talked about the importance of instrumenting your APIs, not only to ensure that they are running as expected but also to convey the value of your API program to stakeholders. An API platform can provide various features for collecting, analyzing, and displaying API related data and metrics to different users or personas.
Ability to extend the platform with various plugins or connectors.	A single API platform cannot include all possible features and capabilities. Plugins or connectors, written in popular programming languages, are supported mechanisms by which developers can extend the functionality of a selected platform. How is this supported? Through APIs!

The extent to which these capabilities are needed is, of course, dependent on the type of APIs in your program. If you are deploying APIs only for internal consumption, then you may not need strong API bundling or monetization capabilities, or sophisticated traffic management. However, some of these features will be needed regardless of your API program type, including support for endpoint management, security, monitoring, and some form of developer portal. The full list of features included could, of course, be quite extensive and detailed. The intent of this chapter is not to provide an exhaustive list (as this will change as technology evolves and be dependent on your needs), but instead describe categories of capabilities that need to be considered in support of your API program and the complete API lifecycle.

There is also, of course, the related topic of build vs. buy, included later in this chapter. Regardless of the approach, supporting your API program and empowering staff to properly manage your APIs is an importance piece of the API puzzle.

Security

Security deserves a separate section because it is so important. It includes the ability to secure API endpoints so only authenticated/authorized API consumers can invoke APIs, and the ability to control who can manage APIs and access related metrics or payloads in the event of a support request or issue.

When dealing with security, there are many questions you should ask yourself to ensure you've considered all the angles. I touched upon this topic in *Chapter 10*, but additional security considerations in the context of API management include:

⇒ *What users and user personas will need to be managed under the API program? What should these users be allowed to do or see?*

⇒ *What roles are there in my program? How will users be grouped into these roles? What should these roles be allowed to do or see?*

⇒ *What security is required for API traffic and communications? TLS? Others?*

⇒ *What security model will be used for API consumer self-service? Trial accounts? And what about for paid customers?*

⇒ *Do I need to consider additional security features such as whitelisting, JWT tokens, call filtering, payload validation, or other security mechanisms?*

⇒ *What is the trade-off between the required security models/features and performance?*

⇒ *How does the API security model filter down or complement the security mechanisms of related back-end systems and services?*

⇒ *Do I need to consider additional topics such as geo-location, regulatory constraints, or certifications?*

The key point that these questions should convey is security is not just about the APIs, it's also about internal users, external consumers, deployment location such as on-premises vs. cloud, industry requirements, data sovereignty, and related back-end systems. Review these considerations carefully, and match these to your choice of API management platform or approach. You do not want to be in the news because of an oversight by short-cutting this part of your program.

Change management

Change management is another topic that has implications for APIs and the various elements that support them. I touched on related topics, such as deprecation in *Chapter 9* and versioning in *Chapter 10*, but change management includes so much more.

When you make a change to your APIs, you need to follow a corresponding set of change management processes. Is the change a "breaking" change? If so, then your strategy for API versioning or evolution will need to be employed. Looking to determine if an API can be deprecated? Again, your change management processes will be engaged to ensure that your customers do not suddenly experience a loss of API capabilities. In both of these situations, API management tools can help ensure the changes are made with the least amount of impact, in a streamlined way, and with a minimum amount of cost.

For example, many API management platforms will provide capabilities for viewing API definition history, facilitating version cutover, and for automating the process of deploying the identified API changes via DevOps techniques. These platforms may also facilitate communicating these changes to your audience through notification mechanisms over various channels or through a developer portal, and provide a centralized location for API consumers to obtain information and provide feedback on upcoming changes or deprecation proposals. The API metrics collected by such platforms are a huge benefit when it comes to prioritizing and evaluating the best changes to make to your API program because they can indicate trends in usage, performance, and other KPIs that will provide input into your decisions.

Of course, changes don't just occur to your APIs—they also occur in other areas that may be directly or indirectly related to your API program. For example, the organizational structure may change, including via the arrival of a new executive, changes to how the business is organized, or through a merger or acquisition. Underlying systems may evolve, including the move of an enterprise system to the cloud, the implementation of a new SaaS service, or the decommissioning of a legacy system. These changes will likely impact your API program. The value of the program may be questioned by the new executive, users may need to be removed or added to the management platform as personnel changes, a set of new capabilities may suddenly need to be migrated to the platform due to an acquisition, or underlying API code may need to be updated to handle underlying system changes. Again, an API management platform and corresponding change management strategy can facilitate these types of changes, limit their impact as much as possible, and balance the need to quickly deploy any identified changes against factors such as cost and risk.

Finally, keep in mind the fact that not only do the APIs need to handle change with little to no downtime, but any deployed API management capabilities also need to be able to handle change. Upgrades, enhancements, configuration changes, and other adjustments need to be carefully considered, so the impact to your API consumers is hidden as much as possible.

APM for APIs

Application Performance Management (APM), is a general industry term typically used to describe "the monitoring and management of performance and availability of software applications."[15] In our case, the phrase "software applications" refers to the APIs, as well

---

[15] https://bit.ly/2WgJH6n.

as to the API management platform that may be used to support an associated monitoring strategy.

Don't forget to include the management platform in your APM framework, along with any underlying dependencies! It is important to recognize that, from an organizational standpoint, APM has been traditionally owned by a centralized IT function or shared ops team within an enterprise. Recently, however, with the popularity of development approaches such as microservices, and with greater focus on the end-user experience, it has become common to have the APM function distributed across the various teams that own logical groupings of APIs and services. Regardless of the structure, any API program needs to be supported with a proper monitoring strategy to ensure the overall health of the program, its users, and subsequent successes.

APM for APIs is typically focused on providing information for two main purposes. The first, of course, is to provide information and metrics on the overall health of the APIs to determine that they are running as expected and to make the API consumer experience the best it can be. The second is related to the business value of the program, as metrics gathered by an APM system may be used to showcase how your APIs are being used, the types of consumers benefiting from them, related ROI values, and which APIs may need to be optimized or are candidates for deprecation.

Lastly, APM for APIs should not be an afterthought. As discussed in *Chapter 9*, monitoring functions and any supporting programmatic hooks should be considered early, and included in the design, implementation, and testing phases of your API. Collect performance-related information from day one, remember to consider any dependent systems or services, and don't forget the KPIs that are important to measuring the success of your API program.

Metrics and reporting

When it comes to metrics and reporting, there are numerous measures and choices available for collecting, displaying, and analyzing related data. These choices can be related to the API consumer, the APIs, the underlying runtime architecture, API dependencies, or general IT infrastructure. There is also the need to consider the audience or personas for these metrics and reports. Will certain metrics be exposed to the API consumers through the developer portal? To an executive team through a set of summary reports or dashboards? To a centralized IT function? Or to individual API teams? And are there any security considerations around the logged data?

Combinations of all of these facets are most likely. Thus it is important to look at each of them during the definition and development of your API program and to provide relevant data where possible.

Given the number of possibilities, in many cases it can be valuable to start small with your implementation, and then grow the sophistication level as experience with the program grows, the number or complexity of your APIs increases, and gaps or common challenges are learned through broader and increased use of your exposed functionality.

API management: build or buy?

The decision to build or buy API management capabilities can be a tough one. You are expected to navigate through the noise often present in the industry. Developers promise that everything can be written for "free" using a combination of code and open source, and everyone seems to have different opinions on which approach or platform is the best. I have seen many instances of "architecture by resume" where the selected tool or approach is not necessarily the right fit for the enterprise, but is the right fit for an individual's next job. A bit harsh perhaps. But this happens, and it is important to recognize early that organizational politics often play a role in platform selection and approach. It is important to minimize this impact and to focus on the requirements, including those needed now and in the future.

If you decide on the "buy" path, there is the typical, simple set of initial criteria. Does the platform or solution meet your needs now, will it continue to do so in the months and years ahead, and will it be done at the right short- and long-term cost? These are obvious, but what are some specific API management platform considerations, or features that should be included in your evaluation?

To help with this question, I find it useful to break the criteria into categories and to assign each with relevant and important capabilities. I've listed some sample categories below and have included a few sample questions—obviously not an exhaustive list, but this will provide a good starting point and set of items to consider and extend.

This list is related to the API management platform features provided at the beginning of this chapter, but builds upon it with broader items and questions. Combining this information is a good start for a platform evaluation, and the resulting answers could even form the basis of an API Management Platform Request for Information (RFI) or Request for Proposal (RFP).

Category	Considerations/Questions
Architecture	Includes questions on general architecture, deployment options, and any related vulnerability or performance testing done by the vendor against the platform. • What deployment options are available? Private cloud, public cloud, containers, hybrid, service mesh? • Describe the overall architecture of the platform, including its ability to scale globally, support high-availability, and meet disaster recovery requirements. • Describe how the platform handles multiple business units sharing the same platform. • How is vulnerability and performance testing done for the platform?
Developer Portal	Covers the capabilities of any provided developer portal, including features for developer onboarding, portal setup and configuration, API testing, API discovery, API documentation, and any supported collaboration and community features. • Does the portal provide capabilities for developer self-service and registration? How are distributed API keys managed? • What levels of access control are provided to limit portal functionality to certain categories of users? • How customizable is the portal, including the ability to extend portal functionality with code or integrations to external systems? • What features does the portal provide for API testing? API discovery and search? For distributing API artifacts such as documentation, SDKs, tutorials, or code snippets? • What collaboration or community features does the portal support?

Category	Considerations/Questions
API Gateway	Describes items specific to APIs, including topics such as API lifecycle management, API plans, configuration management, fault management, traffic management, performance features, routing, and policy definitions. • Describe how the platform supports adding, updating, or deleting API definitions and API consumers. • Describe how the platform supports the entire API lifecycle, from ideation to deprecation. • Does the platform offer features for defining and establishing API plans? • How are API configurations changed after their initial deployment? What impact does this have on API consumers? • How does the platform handle and provide notifications of API errors and exceptions? • Describe the platform's traffic management capabilities. Are features such as quotas, rate limiting, and prioritization supported? • Describe the caching capabilities of the platform. • Describe the platform's ability to support the definition of API policies. • How does the platform support a CI/CD or DevOps process?

Category	Considerations/Questions
Security	Outlines the various security features of the platform, including general security management capabilities, OAuth support, role-based access control (RBAC), SSO, LDAP, access policies, and data privacy. • Describe how the platform manages authentication and authorization API policies. • Outline how the platform approaches API security, including key management, whitelisting/blacklisting, token support, auditing, and access control. • Describe the platform's support for security features such as OAuth, SSO, LDAP, OpenID, and RBAC. • Does the platform support the creation of different security policies for various levels of users or API consumers? • Does the platform support encryption, certificate management, data masking, data filtering, or other data privacy features?
Reporting & Analytics	Covers the APM, reporting, analytics, and logging capabilities of the platform. • Describe how the platform supports the capture of metrics and related monitoring information. What metrics are collected, how are these metrics visualized, and can different access levels and views for these metrics be defined based on user or role? • What analytics are provided by the platform? Does the platform provide out-of-the-box visualizations? How customizable are the reports and analytics? Support for advanced analytics (AI/ML) and real-time analysis? • Describe how the metrics and analytics may be exposed to external tools. • How does the platform support auditing and logging? Does the platform support end-to-end tracing of API calls? What types of audit and system logs are captured and exposed by the platform? How are these secured?

Category	Considerations/Questions
API Monetization	Considers how the platform may support the monetization of your APIs. Typically includes questions on the types of metrics collected to support monetization, as well as its ability to support various pricing models and integrate with external customer and billing systems.
API Development	Covers the platform's capabilities when it comes to API development, including the ability to design API contracts/schemas, route and transform calls/data, version APIs, perform API choreography, support different API implementation patterns (e.g. request/reply, async, service mesh), and host different types of API endpoints. • Describe how the platform supports the process of designing different types of APIs, including the generation of mock apps. • What types of routing are supported by the platform? Content-based routing? Rule or analytics-based? Version routing? • What types of transformations are supported? Formats and protocols? Data transformations? • How is versioning and deprecation supported by the platform? • Is API choreography supported? Integration to external systems? • What types of APIs may be managed by the platform? REST? Web services? GraphQL? What associated standards are supported?
Support & Maintenance	Describes the support options and associated costs, along with any additional maintenance fees. Typically outlines how new features are released, and the process for performing platform upgrades.

Category	Considerations/Questions
Licensing and Pricing	Presents the various ways in which the platform may be purchased and deployed. May include various options depending on the number of APIs/API consumers, deployment location (for example, containers, on-premises), or whether the platform software is being used via a SaaS or subscription model.

Final thoughts

In the end, the big question still to be answered is, do you build or buy? This comes down to the importance and priority of the capabilities above, the culture of the organization, your core competency, your desire to build something that may already exist, total cost vs. savings, and any special needs or considerations. I didn't say it was going to be easy! But hopefully this chapter gives you a good place to start.

CHAPTER 14

APIs for the Long Haul

An API program is not an initiative with a clear end; it should become a living part of your digital infrastructure and adapt as customer needs, target markets, and your industry change. You should review your API program for success regularly, and look for opportunities to expand it to address new audiences and capabilities. This chapter explains how, and concludes this guide.

In this chapter, you'll learn what to include as you regularly review your APIs, and how to measure the success and health of your API program. I will also share some interesting developments on the horizon that you'll want to watch as you look for opportunities to grow and improve your program.

Review for continuous success

As presented throughout this book, APIs are an enabler of innovation for your organization and API consumers. From hiding the complexities of underlying legacy systems to enabling the rapid assembly of new business capabilities, APIs can form the foundation upon which massive amounts of value can be unleashed. But simply creating and deploying APIs is not enough—a successful API program must have an associated support and continuous improvement process, and also be aligned to the goals of the business. A set of KPIs for evaluating the success of your API program is important, but it is possible to measure the wrong things.

Focus on metrics that represent the business initiatives of your organization, and the investment you have made in your API program will be properly reflected.

For example, measuring factors such as the number of deployed APIs, direct API program costs, and number of API customers are not always the best measures of API value. Simply having more APIs does not mean you are providing the right value to your API consumers, and having more APIs can be detrimental when it comes to maintaining high levels of program quality. Secondly, while it is important to understand the cost of your API program, it can be difficult to determine an exact direct value. APIs often indirectly reduce the costs of other initiatives inside of your organization, and they will, of course, also impact the costs (and revenue) of your API consumers. Thus, basing the success of your program purely on cost can be misleading. Lastly, having a large number of API consumers is also not necessarily an indicator of success. How many of those consumers are active? Are they driving more or less traffic? What is the associated support cost for these consumers compared to the value they are generating?

More accurate measures of API program success typically include metrics such as the growth in API traffic, number of active API consumers, and the level of reuse inside and outside your organization. Steady growth in API traffic can indicate that your target audience is increasingly using your APIs, and business value is being realized as a result. A growing number of active API consumers (the key point here is, they are active) is also often a good indicator of the value your APIs are providing, along with increases in the frequency of access or calls. Finally, KPIs that reflect the level of API reuse, speed of developing new APIs and associated business functions, and the impact (often indirect) to customer satisfaction and cost/revenue, can also be very helpful when establishing the value of your program. Take note of these metrics, track them over time, and be sure to communicate what they are indicating to key stakeholders and partners. If the numbers swing wildly, go negative, or become stagnant for some period, take a step back and re-evaluate your metrics, investigate underlying root causes, and make necessary adjustments to your program.

The API health check-up

Whether monthly, quarterly, bi-annually, or yearly, as part of an API continuous improvement process, a regularly scheduled "health check-up" for your API program is recommended. Its frequency somewhat depends on how quickly your program is evolving, and on its maturity, but regardless of the timing, regular reviews are important to API program success.

In addition to the KPIs discussed above, check-ups typically cover the health of the API program technology, a review of the original business case, and the effectiveness of the materials created to support your API consumers. See *Chapter 5* for details on how to justify an API program and *Chapter 12* for a discussion of the recommended materials and processes. Identify the APIs that need attention, review associated KPIs and success metrics, incorporate feedback as needed, and, most importantly, ensure everything is up to date. This is also a great time to review the organizational structure of your API program and ensure it still meets the needs of the business.

To help with this check-up, look at questions that can assist with assessing how your platform is serving you today, how it was established, and where it needs to go. The following list of questions can be used as a starting point—hopefully you can take these and adapt them to a set which best fits your needs. Combine these with your

KPIs, and you will have an effective approach for evaluating your API program.

Category	Questions
Overall Business Goals	• What does API success look like for you? • What are the business drivers for your APIs? • What are the expectations for the program? • What other APIs in the market do you see as comparable success stories?
Scope and Timeline	• What does the current and future program and API product roadmap look like? • Are the data, content, and services already in existence? • How are new features being prioritized?
Value Proposition	• What makes your APIs unique? • How do your APIs compare to other APIs in the industry? • What features are you delivering based on immediate internal or external consumer needs?
Target Partners and Applications	• Who is waiting for your APIs? • Who do you want to be working with your APIs? • What applications do you expect to be successful with your APIs? • Do you have any plans to open these APIs to the wider developer public, such as through open ecosystems, hackathons, or startups?

Category	Questions
Target Developer Audience	• Who will use your APIs? • On what platforms do they commonly develop? • What is their existing API experience? • How will you reach out to them? • How will you respond to their needs?
Internal Landscape	• Who are the program's key sponsors? • How is the API program currently viewed? • What are the potential or existing obstacles? • How much does the program need to be championed within the organization?
Team and Resources	• Who is in place to drive the APIs and program? • Who can promote/market the APIs? • Who can support the development of the APIs? • Are you willing to hire the resources that are needed? Do you have adequate staffing levels for the needed API roles?
Technical Knowledge	• Who is the technical lead for the program? • What is the team's level of knowledge and experience with API architectures and interfaces? • What areas of knowledge need research? • How will this knowledge be gained?
Resource and Object Discovery	• What resources/objects need to be exposed to best serve your business goals? • What functions, methods, and properties should be enacted upon them? • Who should have access to those resources and their data?

Category	Questions
API Contract Considerations	• What standards and approaches are used by your competitors or partners?
	• With what standards or approaches is your target audience most comfortable?
	• What standards and capabilities can your current infrastructure support? What will be needed?
Infrastructure Considerations	• How much capacity do you have? On-premises? Cloud? Containers? Other platforms?
	• How quickly can you scale?
	• What are your plans for growth in the next 3/6/12/24 months?
	• How are you creating these APIs?

This list of topics is meant as a starting point for your own health check-up or assessment. Some of these may seem unnecessary, especially for programs that have been running for some time. However, it does not hurt to re-evaluate the basics. Perform a check-up regularly, be relatively formal, and generate a set of items upon which you can act.

What's next for APIs?

Like everything else in the world today, APIs will continue to rapidly evolve and change. Use of APIs will expand and grow in strength and value, and associated technology will adapt as required. API development techniques, libraries, coding frameworks, platforms, and best practices will continue to be debated, and more endpoints will be exposed as companies realize the promise of their API programs.

As part of this rapid evolution, there are definitely some interesting API related topics worth watching. As always, don't just jump into these areas without some research and investigation. However, it is important to be aware of trends in the world of APIs, and to test some of these features or usage patterns in an innovation lab within your organization. Given the pace of change and the rate of digital transformation occurring in every industry, a slight delay in the identification and adoption of a new capability can result in falling behind the competition—don't let this be you!

For example, at the moment, the topic of APIs is being discussed in conjunction with the following areas.

- **Internet of Things (IoT) / Industrial IoT (IIoT).** The use of IoT and the creation of massively distributed systems is driving the use of APIs not just in the cloud or data center, but at the edge as well. Useful for creating abstraction layers on top of low-level device interfaces, and for supporting the exposure and management of IoT endpoints, APIs are being deployed in both a request/reply and streaming context when it comes to the world of devices and IoT.

- **Artificial Intelligence/Machine Learning (AI/ML)**. In data science, APIs play a critical role. From exposing generated data science models to external consumers, to allowing users to consume data from one or more sources through a set of API-based abstraction layers, APIs are key to exposing the capabilities needed for a successful analytics lifecycle and data fabric strategy. And, when it comes to APIs you have deployed, their usage and traffic may also provide interesting insights into an organization when analyzed with AI/ML techniques. For example, applying pattern analysis techniques against API traffic may point out areas or times of abnormal access, which in turn may indicate attempts at fraud or other malicious activity. Lastly, as organizations move to more advanced self-service analytics environments, APIs will play a critical role in enabling the discovery and retrieval of key data assets.

- **Events and Event-driven Architecture**. APIs are no longer just about request/reply over HTTP. As organizations rediscover the advantages of events and event-driven architecture patterns, APIs will also need to support the use and management of event-driven endpoints across the architecture. As previously mentioned, the AsyncAPI (https://www.asyncapi.com/) initiative is an attempt to create a specification that makes it easier to work with this style of API, and projects such as CloudEvents (https://cloudevents.io/) are also emerging to facilitate the exchange of events and event data between systems.

- **Extended Reality**. As the world looks to technology related to Augmented Reality, Mixed Reality, and Virtual Reality for new and exciting ways to interact with data and a person's surroundings, APIs can play a supporting role. Associated devices can use APIs to get their needed data (using both request/reply and real-time access patterns), and any user interactions can trigger actions and commands that are again exposed by APIs.

- **Blockchain**. Looking beyond the hype, the technology and concepts behind enterprise blockchains have some interesting uses when it comes to building decentralized business networks with a certain degree of trust, automation, and security. Regardless of how this area evolves, the value of such networks is becoming more prevalent as organizations realize they need to build and participate in expanded value chains to improve their products and services. Blockchain, however, does not exist by itself. Other applications, for example, need to interact with these decentralized business networks to trigger certain functions or to obtain information. How is this best done? APIs can be the answer.

- **Autonomic Computing and Intelligent Agents.** Topics such as autonomic computing, intelligent software agents, and belief-desire-intent (BDI) software models are areas of research that seek to combine concepts such as events, analytical models, state, and time into distributed systems that can act together with minimal (or no) human involvement. While a discussion of these topics is outside the scope of this book, the use of APIs to support these lightweight distributed agents is a logical step.

Emerging industry standards

APIs, of course, are not just about what you define and build within the walls of your organization. The importance and value of APIs are also prevalent across many third-party agencies as different industries look to improve interoperability and standardize the APIs used for common business functions and information exchanges. Standards, specifications, and approaches for APIs are emerging in a number of industries—examples from industries such as finance, healthcare, and transportation/logistics are noted below.

- **Open Banking** (https://bit.ly/2AZHUdB). Open Banking is "the secure way to give providers access to your financial information." Among other things, Open Banking standards "contain the specifications to securely connect regulated third party apps and websites to account providers using APIs. And because regulated third party providers and account providers use the same specifications, one solution works for customers of many different banks and building societies."

- **New Distribution Capability** (https://bit.ly/3dvssE1). New Distribution Capability ". . . is a travel industry-supported program (**NDC Program**) launched by IATA for the development and market adoption of a new, XML-based data transmission standard (**NDC Standard**)."

- **FHIR** (https://bit.ly/2LcYXuv). Fast Healthcare Interoperability Resources (FHIR) "is a next generation standards framework created by HL7. FHIR combines the best features of HL7's v2, HL7 v3 and CDA product lines while leveraging the latest web standards and applying a tight focus on implementability."

The emergence of these standards is another growing area within the industry and something to monitor within your own vertical to ensure you support the approaches and technologies relevant (and potentially mandated) to your API consumers.

Final thoughts

Throughout this book, it should be obvious the API journey is a long one, and the successful program is one that is business-driven, continuous, and adequately supported. When done right, APIs can form the core foundation for a flexible architecture that can sustain true innovation, both now and in the future. There is no one way to look at APIs because there are many related strategies and value points, but it is my hope this book has provided you with some guidance for your journey and will serve you well even as technologies and trends change over time.

Thanks for coming along with me! I'm looking forward to hearing more about your API successes in the marketplace. Happy "API-ing"!

Index

Printed in Great Britain
by Amazon

35234052R00185